TIME, SPACE AND THE MIND

Dr. Irving Oyle

CELESTIAL ARTS
Millbrae, California

First Printing, November 1976
Made in the United States of America

Library of Congress Cataloging in Publication Data

Oyle, Irving, 1925–
    Time, space, and the mind.

    1. Mental healing.   2. Mind and body
3. Space and time.   I. Title
RZ401.085   615'.851   76-11339
ISBN 0-89087-122-1

        5 6 7 8 – 81

Contents

For Julie and Fred
For Abby and Ben
For Darla Mae
and her bears in their den

Foreword

"You Americans are about fifty years behind the times in your practice of medicine. You completely ignore the work and theories of Albert Einstein." This remark, made by a Russian physicist, suggests the obsolescence of our approach to disease.

Most of us see our body as a moving lump of matter which is acted upon by malefic forces or energies. The result of this incursion is disease. These forces—germs, poisons, etc., are conceived to be outside of, and different from, the body which they invade. This approach is a direct outgrowth of the Newtonian idea that a billiard ball and the energy which moves it are two separate entities. The Newtonian scientist regards his or her observing consciousness as distinctly different from either the billiard ball or the force which causes it to move. In a like manner, the mind of a patient is seen as disconnected from the matter of the body, and separate from the energy which "causes" illness.

Our Russian colleague refers to the statement of Professor Einstein that $E = MC^2$. This revolutionary allegation suggests that matter and energy are two aspects of a single phenomenon, one convertible into the other: The constant factor (C) which connects the phenomena of mass (M) and energy (E) being the speed of light.

Light itself is now said to exist in two mutually exclusive forms. It can manifest as a particle which has mass (M), or as a wave, which is pure energy (E). In a recent report, the late Dr. Joseph Bronowski offered a useful analogy to illustrate the interrelationship between mass, energy and velocity which is proposed by Einstein's theory of relativity.

Imagine a tram which has the ability to move at the speed of light. Picture yourself onboard. As your speed accelerates, you will notice that the buildings in the city outside seem to be undergoing a physical change. The faster you go, the taller and thinner they become. As the tram increases its speed, the buildings lose all definitive shape, becoming a formless blur, and finally disappear completely as you attain the speed of light.

The same event as seen by an observer on the street would create a totally different subjective experience. If you placed yourself in front of one of the buildings, you would note that the tram itself becomes taller and thinner as its speed increases. If it passed your vantage point at the speed of light, you would see nothing since, for you, all the matter of the tram and its contents would cease to exist; as the street and its occupants would cease to exist for the passenger on the tram. The matter of each has been converted into energy from the *point of view* of the other. A simple way to observe the direct transformation of matter into energy is to watch a burning log disappear.

The idea of the identity of energy and matter has enormous implications for all the healing professions. It gives us a theoretical basis from which to consider therapeutic methods such as acupuncture which purport to restore normal bodily states by manipulating the flow of cosmic energy. If energy and matter are indeed complementary states of a single entity, perhaps it is not unreasonable to hypothesize that by attention to the energy level, we can effect changes in the matter of the physical body.

Dr. V. Inyushin, a noted Russian physicist, offers for our consideration the theory of "Bioplasmic Energy." His hypothesis suggests that there is a single energy permeating our entire universe. He visualizes this energy (which he calls *bioplasma*) manifesting as a flow of subatomic particles such as photons, gravitons, neutrinos, positrons, electrons, etc. Many of these particles, which by their interactions create atoms and the known physical world, have not been demonstrated to exist physically. We know them only by the tracks they leave in our particle detectors. They may be said to exist only in our minds. Professor Inyushin feels that the *bioplasma* enters the living human body through acupuncture points in the skin. He seems to accept the old Chinese acupuncture meridian system through which cosmic energy is purported to flow, the bioplasma corresponding to *Chi* (the ancient Chinese term for universal or cosmic energy). He is specifically postulating the existence of a fourth circulatory system within the human body—as did the yellow Emperor's physician. (Since the ancient Chinese also discovered the usefulness of the silk worm and invented the compass, it would seem to make sense that we think twice before looking down our noses at their medical model.)

A tremendous advance was made by the healing professions after William Harvey led them, kicking and screaming, to the realization that blood flows through a closed circulatory system. Although he is considered by many as the founder of modern medicine, his revolutionary "circulatory *system*" was not fully accepted and substantiated for more than 200 years.

The notion that bodily energies flow through invisible channels opens vistas of enormous magnitude to the mind of the scientist who will merely *consider* it. The destructive energies released in the world by nuclear fission may be equaled in magnitude by the healing effects of applying $E = MC^2$ therapeutically. Constructive versus destructive aspects of energy, (i.e., acupuncture therapeutics as opposed to the atomic bomb) are merely two aspects of one single power—its opposite poles.

To bolster Dr. Inyushin's theory, Dr. Victor Adamenko of the Moscow Institute of Radiotechnology has described work indicating that the acupuncture points on the human skin show uniformly decreased electrical resistance. He described them as electrical windows in the skin. The acupuncture points "suck in" or "absorb" energy much the same as "black holes" in outer space are said to suck in particles; by creating a whirlpool or downward spiraling motion.

Dr. Inyushin also reported research at the medical center at Kazakh State University where he heads the department of physics. Selected acupuncture points in a patient with osteosarcoma of the leg were stimulated by a beam of low intensity laser light . . . just enough to cause redness of the skin. Regression of the tumor and subsequent regrowth of normal bone were observed following this procedure.

Later, during informal conversation, I asked Dr. Inyushin if he thought vibratory energy in the frequency ranges constituting sound and ultrasound might be as effective as laser light. He agreed that it was worth looking into. Results of the research that ensued and the data obtained in early experiments were published as an article in *The Osteopathic Physician*, September, 1973, which is reprinted in Chapter III in its entirety. The definitive report on this work is to be found in my earlier book, *The Healing Mind*.

As we enter the last quarter of the twentieth century we find that Western consciousness is experiencing something that may be adequately described as an apocalypse. Alvin Toffler touched on this concept in his highly provocative book, *Future Shock*. Long cherished guidelines such as motherhood, fatherland, chastity, God, and the like, flap uselessly, buffeted and torn asunder by the winds of violent change. Paradigms, personal opinions, and common sense notions are crumbling under a torrent of new information spewing out of computers at the speed of light.

It is the purpose of this book to provide a bridge between what you, the reader, believe to be the down-to-earth, day-to-day, real world, and the mind-created world of the particle physicist. To provide a series of stepping-stones from there to here—to take you from where you are so that, through reading and comprehending the material presented, your view of reality is examined, and by this examination, changed.

This book, like your brain, is divided into two halves. Part One speaks to your left brain; more specifically, it addresses itself to your left cerebral hemisphere. The left side of your head is where you store your speech center. It is this brain half which runs the right side of your body. It stores information in a logical, linear, rational mode. In our particular Western culture, it thinks it knows all there is to know . . . about everything. This left sided reasoning mind is the source and the storehouse for the widespread Western prejudice against things like hunches, visions, dreams, and other forms of irrational thought.

For the purposes of our discussion, I will arbitrarily designate the left cerebral hemispheric consciousness as male. He is represented symbolically by the male side of the alchemical winged hermaphrodite, and by the light yang side of the Eastern yin yang totality symbol. Reason has served humanity well; he must be treated with respect. Part One is presented for his considered attention.

Part Two is for the edification of your right brained feminine side. The right half of the human brain processes information in a nonlinear, nonanalytical mode. She has the ability to take in a series of apparently disconnected data bits and put them together in a new form. It is she who sees the face on the moon or on the barroom floor. Part Two is meant to be read and experienced. Do not try to analyze or judge it on the basis of belief systems which you currently hold. The "hook" which ties the images together is the fact they inhabit the same consciousness. Some of the pictures arose from my own sense experience; they came from out there, the real world. Others were stimulated by a rapidly moving beam of electrons entering my eyes from a color television set. Still others were word pictures describing someone else's experience (newspaper stories). A large group had no origin in time and space. They arose spontaneously from my own right brain. This, of course, does not make them any less real, since I actually saw them in my mind's eye, and as we all know, seeing is believing. It is my hope that through this shared trip you will learn to feel natural and comfortable in your own total experience; to relax, enjoy, and to learn firsthand that the whole is always greater than the sum of its parts.

PART ONE: FOR OSIRIS
Your Left Cerebral Hemisphere

"Miracles are not contrary to nature. They are only contrary to what (we think) we know about nature."

St. Augustine, A.D. 333

The Nameless Dreads

Much of the skepticism and prejudice which first greeted the data reported by acupuncture therapy researchers in the mid-1960s had two bases. First, the idea that sticking a needle into the foot can alleviate the symptoms of a painful tooth infection is sheer nonsense from the reality viewpoint of the twentieth century allopathic (drug oriented) medical establishment. "It doesn't make sense," is the same as saying "It isn't real," or, "It didn't happen."

Proponents of this point of view have developed a rather quaint theory to explain the anesthetic and healing effects demonstrated by various acupuncturists in the U. S. and abroad. In the case of pain relief, they suggest that the patient was merely distracted by the procedure. Through something called *hypnosis*, the patient ceases to feel the pain which, we are assured, persists despite the fact that nobody feels it. Faced with patient claims which suggest that major maladies have been relieved or even cured by acupuncture, we are told (with a knowing smile) that the diseases "cured" by this method were not real. The patients only imagined they were sick, so obviously, they only think they were cured. This Rube Goldberg type of explanation is another way of saying that the therapeutic results reported by acupuncturists and their patients aren't real. They are not considered real because we know of no *mechanism* by which twirling a needle in the hand produces sufficient anesthesia to permit the surgical removal of a lung.

The essential point made by many American critics is that

3

the patients were caused to hallucinate pain relief and symptom alleviation through a quasi-occult practice called *hypnosis*. If we follow this line of reasoning, we would have to ascribe all proven non-drug induced cures of human illness to *magic*. Magic is an event which we cannot explain and which therefore arouses in us a disease which I would like to name: *The Nameless Dreads*; specifically, a subjective experience of unreasoning, animal-like fear in the face of anything not explainable by the victim's rational mind. It is the unquestionable basis for the outright rejection of data which in any way challenges our concept of what is real.

Victims of *The Nameless Dreads*, highly esteemed by contemporary medical orthodoxy, scoffed at the drawings of William Harvey, who proposed that blood flows in channels or vessels as we discussed earlier. They hounded the alchemist, Paracelsus, all over Europe (we will examine his contempt for traditional theories later and at length). These same logic oriented medical men told Semmelweis he was insane. It was he who audaciously suggested to highly credentialed surgeons of his time that the reason so many young women were dying in childbirth was related to the fact that the eminent physicians who were delivering them never washed their hands. They saw no rational reason why they could not go directly to the delivery room from the men's room or the autopsy table without first performing some ridiculous, superstitious hand-washing ritual.

It is interesting to compare this attitude with those being expressed in dressing rooms and dining rooms in many hospitals during the current era of Marcus Welby, M. D. Today's conventional wisdom calls symptom relief after drug administration a *cure*. The same event, restoration of health, following acupuncture, prayer, laying on of hands, visual imagery, biofeedback, hypnotic suggestion, or any other ritual is call a *healing*. This choice of words indicates the former is real while the latter is unreal, and therefore suspect. An editor for *The New York Times* refused to review *The Healing Mind* because, he said, "I don't believe in healing."

Werner Erhardt of *e.s.t.* says, "Belief is a disease." The physician William James, in his *Varieties of Religious Experience*, makes the following pertinent observation: "An idea (belief) can galvanize the believer's entire being even though it has no existence. It colors our entire experience of material reality."

An idea with the power to alter our entire experience of material reality is called a *paradigm* by the modern scientific community, an *archetype* by Jungian psychiatrists, and an *idea* by the followers of the dead Greek named Plato. The *ideas* which set the tone for the quality of human existence on the planet Earth are deceptively simple; even childish. Let us examine one. Are you a pessimist or an optimist? That is, *do you believe that the universe which you inhabit is indifferent to your existence and well being? Or, do you believe that the cosmos, our galaxy and our solar system are specifically designed to further your own personal growth, happiness, and evolution?*

A story called *The Lady or the Tiger* is relevant. It concerns a young man who was caught in bed with the queen, by the king. An absolute monarch with a penchant for games of chance, his majesty made our hero an offer he couldn't refuse. In order to provide an entertainment for his court, he ordered the hapless lad placed in a bullring which had two doors. "You may open either door. Behind one, is a ravenous two-thousand pound Bengal tiger. Behind the other, a beautiful maiden." The king then leaned over and whispered the following: "You will be either torn to pieces or married on the spot . . . the odds are fifty fifty. The queen, our joint bed partner, knows what lies behind each door." Glancing up at the lady, the young man saw her point to the door on the right. Unhesitatingly he opened it. Which came out, the tiger or the lady?

Your honest, gut level answer to this koan indicates which of the above paradigms rule your own individual existence. Borrowing labels made popular by Doctors Friedman and Rosenman with the publication of their book, *Type A Behavior & Your Heart*, we might say that Type A people basically mistrust the cosmos. However, if you espouse the optimistic point of view, you may be considered a Type B person.

The Type A lifestyle engendered by presuming the indifference if not the downright malevolence of the universe and its forces of nature is well described in the following excerpt from *Voices of Freedom* by H. W. Dresser:

"Consider for a moment the habits of life into which we are born. There are certain social conventions or customs . . . a theological bias, a general view of the world [universe]. There are [rigid] ideas in regard to our early training, our education, marriage, and occupation in life. Following close upon this, there is a long series of anticipations, namely that we shall suffer certain children's diseases, diseases of middle life, and of old age; the thought that we shall grow old, and lose our faculties. Crowning all this is the fear of death. Then there is a long line of particular fears and trouble-bearing expectancies . . . ideas about certain kinds of foods, the dread of the east wind, the terrors of hot weather, the aches and pains associated with cold weather, the fear of catching cold if one sits in a draft, the coming of hayfever season, and so on through a long list of fears, dreads, worriments, anxieties, anticipations, expectations, pessimisms, morbidities, and the whole ghostly train of fateful shapes which our fellow men especially physicians are ready to help us conjure up. Yet," he continues, "this is not all. This vast array is swelled by innumerable volunteers from daily life: fear of accident, the possibility of calamity, the loss of property, the chance of robbery, of fire, or the outbreak of war."

Written in 1899, this description is equally valid almost a century later. Humans who see themselves living in an indifferent, alien universe, are bound to pass their lives in a state of chronic anxiety and fear. The subjective manifestations of this state are those of the disease entity, *The Nameless Dreads*.

One Henry Wood (a contemporary of H. W. Dresser, quoted by Dr. James in *Varieties of Religious Experience*) gives the following vivid description of a victim suffering

The Nameless Dreads: ''(The) Man has fear stamped upon him; he is reared in fear . . . all his life is passed in bondage to fear of disease and death . . . his whole mentality becomes cramped, limited and depressed, and his body follows its shrunken pattern and specification.'' Seventy-five years after this particular description, we find *The Nameless Dreads* manifesting in epidemic proportions in Western society. This disease entity (which, you recall, one gets from embracing the idea that the universe doesn't give a damn whether you live or die) manifests in the mind of the patient as chronic anxiety and depression. The bodily state induced by this disease has been called by Dr. Hans Selye the state of *chronic alarm.* The chronic alarm condition is usually described and experienced by the patient as a ''gnawing'' in the pit of the stomach or a ''tightness'' in the chest.

''How,'' you may ask, ''can an *idea,* an ephemeral nothing, gnaw at my stomach and constrict my chest?''

''Polarizing and magnetizing us as they do,'' responds Dr. James, ''we turn towards them and from them, we seek them, hold them, hate them, bless them, just as if they were so many concrete beings. And beings they are, beings as real in the realm which they inhabit as the changing things of sense are in the realm of (time and) space.''

''That's all very fine,'' counters the hard-nosed realist, ''but what is the *mechanism* by which these nonexistent beings (ideas) affect my *real* body?'' Modern medical theory holds that ideas manifest in the brain as patterns of electrochemical activity. That is to say that we conceive of them as somehow connected with brain waves, and with the flow of electricity which we can measure in the nerves of the cerebral cortex. An idea which carries an emotional charge of energy is called an *opinion.* A rigidly crystallized opinion carries a higher emotional charge and is called a *belief.* The energy is carried by connecting nerves to the pituitary gland in the center of the skull. The pituitary is the master gland of the endocrine system; a group of glands which secrete directly into the bloodstream. The hormones which they exude are the most powerfully active drugs known to man.

Examining the brain-pituitary-endocrine gland axis, we find that specific ideas are faithfully transformed into objectively identifiable bodily states. The mere idea that I am confronted in the real world by something which threatens my existence translates itself instantaneously into a squirt of adrenaline; the general alarm which informs every cell of the body that a fight or flight situation exists. The heart cells respond at once by beating wildly in order to divert huge amounts of vital blood to the muscles and away from the exposed and vulnerable skin. The muscles, for their part, are poised and ready to move in any given direction. All this happens at the *idea* that there *might be* a tiger in the bush. It does not require a real tiger to set off the physiologic events we call the fight or flight reaction. The intensity of the reaction is directly proportional to the energy charge contained in the *idea*. As the power in the idea mounts from an opinion to a belief to a certainty, the physiologic manifestations of that idea increase in intensity. The victim feels the effects of adrenaline secretion (contracted chest musculature and rapidly beating heart) as a tightness in the chest. The restriction of breathing in many cases of *The Nameless Dreads* occasions a drop in the total available oxygen level in the lung sacs. This is interpreted by the body as a possible threat to life. In turn, it signals the brain that there is indeed a possible threat to existence from some quarter, occasioning another squirt of adrenaline which continues the vicious cycle. The General Adaptation Syndrome accompanies this series of events by release of the hormone cortisone, which is notorious for its ability to gnaw holes in the stomach.

It is through this mechanism that the *idea* that our universe somehow means us harm could engender what we today call the diseases of stress: cancer, stroke, heart disease, and mental depression. An inhabitant of the planet Earth who embraces the idea that it is his lot to contend against the natural forces of our cosmos must take careful note of the price being paid by the body.

Type A people are those who assume *the indifference or outright malevolence of the cosmos*. Today's board-certified specialists still see themselves as somehow interposed between the patient and the blind, destructive forces spawned by a mindless universe. Today they hurl compound after toxic compound at a rising sea of disease entities which do not respond to their skillfully applied therapeutics. In 1976 people are still dying like flies and getting progressively more crazy in our best hospitals. In spite of raging epidemics of diseases of stress, diseases of the aged, venereal diseases, etc., they still insist that their patients are things which must be treated by other *things* (drugs, scalpels, cobalt bombs, etc.).

Patients, for their part, come to the doctor and ask him to give them something which will overcome the consequences of their mental attitude toward life. This is a mistake. Forced relaxation is contrary to reason.

All this continues in spite of the Hippocratic admonition: "ABOVE ALL, DO NO HARM." All this in the face of Einstein's $E = MC^2$: matter and energy are one and the same.

Let us take a closer look at one of the common sequelae or long term effects of *The Nameless Dreads*. We have already seen how they can cause stomach ulcers by the continuous excretion of cortisone for long periods of time. Type A people, faced as they believe themselves to be, by an omnipotent and ever-present enemy, are understandably nervous and excitable. They are constantly squirting adrenaline and cortisone into themselves in response to an endless procession of fear-filled thoughts. They see a potential tiger behind every bush, danger in every new situation. They buy all kinds of insurance, observe every known precaution, but like Macbeth, they do not rest easy. The energy engendered by pictures and thoughts of potential dangers, possible failures and imminent disasters is carried through the nerves in the brain from the cortex, which thinks, down the spinal cord and out to all vital organs by a network of nerves called the sympathetic nervous system. It is through the sympathetic nerves that the worriments of Type A's transform themselves into the phenomenon of sweaty palms. This common symptom indicates a strong flow of energy. A message is being flashed to all vital organs in the body. The message succinctly stated is "Watch your ass!"

Releasing adrenaline at their end points, sympathetic nerves induce the blood vessels supplying major body systems and organs to contract. The preservation of blood is a first priority in any fight or flight situation. They will maintain this state of spasm until they receive the "all clear" signal from the thinking brain in the form of an equally potent message over the wires of the complementary parasympathetic or maintenance nervous system. If the body mechanism is commanded by a Calvinist, nose-to-the grindstone, work ethic which considers relaxation equivalent to copping out, the all clear never comes. Failing to receive an all clear from a nervous commander who thinks the universe is out to get him (her), the blood vessels remain contracted, and constantly maintain an abnormally high blood pressure. Beating against increased pressure, under the brutal whipping of a never ending stream of adrenaline from both nerve impulses and hormonal release, the heart begins to fail. Deprived of vital blood by the relentlessly decreasing caliber of the conduits, the heart and brain respond with "heart attack" and "stroke."

Twentieth century medical orthodoxy insists that the best approach to the syndrome of hypertensive cardiovascular disease consists of interrupting the flow of adrenaline. In common use in the fifties and sixties was a drug called reserpine which lowered the blood pressure and calmed the psyche. The only problem was its nasty tendency to induce malignant, suicidal depression which was unresponsive to any form of treatment. Standard antidotes to the depressive side effects of reserpine were more drugs and electric shock therapy (shooting an electric current into the victim's brain to induce convulsions).

Another group of compounds, called ganglionic blockers, tried to bring blood pressure down by interrupting the nerve impulses along the sympathetic nervous system. They could bring it down, but they made urination difficult, and sex practically impossible. As a last resort, a group of eminently respectable board-certified surgeons were recommending and performing a procedure called a sympathectomy. This technique, which required an inordinate amount of surgical skill, consisted of ripping out large parts of the sympathetic nervous system by means of a long, dangerous, and expensive operation. The most skillful were combining this idiocy with an adrenelectomy in which they tore out the patient's adrenal glands in order to discourage the poor devil from secreting excess adrenaline.

In the past two or three years, research centers in the U. S. and in Europe are reporting that simple meditation will significantly lower blood pressure for prolonged periods of time. Drugs and surgery as treatment for hypertension are dangerous and obsolete if these reports are true.

Since a cure without a known mechanism is a mere healing, let us consider a possible mechanism by which meditation can lower blood pressure where all else has failed. We may safely hypothesize that meditation, which is characterized by the alpha state, induces a condition in which you stop thinking. This cuts off the flow of nerve impulses to the pituitary and the sympathetic nerves at its source . . . halting the *idea* from initiating an endless stream of morbid thoughts. The blood pressure drops as the alarm falls silent; blood vessels, the heart, and the total physical organism relax. As a family physician, I would today urge my patients to have a go at some form of meditation for a reasonable period of time before they undertake any of the currently standard and approved treatments for high blood pressure.

What decides whether one is a Type A or Type B? Is it a matter of blind chance, a whim of mindless fate as expressed in a random arrangement of invisible genes? Was Sigmund Freud on to something when he suggested that the traumatic experience of birth somehow left its mark in the form of a Type A paranoia? The American psychoanalyst and founder of primal scream therapy, Arthur Janov, along with the French obstetrician, Frederick LeBoyer, agree that the birth experience leaves a deep and lasting imprint on the adult.

Religion may play a part. The true believer in Jehovah who smote repeatedly his faithful servant Job, just to show him who was boss, is more likely to be sympathicotonic (in a chronic fight or flight state). The devout Christian who fervently believes that "Christ loves me personally . . . He even died for me . . . He wouldn't hurt me," would tend more naturally to a Type B world view. The physical body state among natives of cultures which believe in an ultimately beneficent deity reflects this relaxed attitude.

The Buddhist view that empirical reality is an illusion continuously created by the mind for your own personal enjoyment and enlightenment is a typical Type B idea. Its Type A counterpart which we call cartesian scientific materialism sums up the human condition thusly; "It's all mindless matter, and it doesn't give a shit about you, so watch your ass."

According to the author of a newspaper article entitled "The Wisdom of Keeping Still" (*San Francisco Examiner* 11/2/75), "This idea goes back to the tap root of our Judeo-Christian heritage." Solomon himself, in Proverbs 24:33, summed it up with this warning: "A little sleep, a little slumber, a little folding of the hands to rest, and poverty will come upon you like a robber, and want like an armed man." A somewhat later philosopher echoed the same thought when he said, "Never look over your shoulder, someone may be gaining on you." This ancient and venerable idea, regardless of its intrinsic merit, may be the prime instigator of what we today call the diseases of stress . . . which run rampant through our society. A good antidote may be the admonition of Christ in the New Testament to "consider the lillies of the field," as an example of the ultimate beneficence of the universe (God). The hypertensive Christian who accepts the Sermon on the Mount at face value, or who even agrees to consider its implications for his or her personal life, must in doing so sound the "all clear" throughout the physical body.

One may be struck by a certain similarity in attitude as expressed in these words and the oriental position which states: "I will do nothing . . . I will be fond of keeping still." This course of action through nonaction presumes a universe which is cyclic, predictable, and ultimately benign. "There is a natural rhythm to the world and the wise man accepts that rhythm." Taoist belief teaches that "misfortune is simply the opposite side of good fortune." They taught that opposites (good and evil, yin and yang, up and down, manic depressive, fat years and lean years, boom and bust, etc.) behave according to the pattern elucidated by the primal opposites, dark and light.

Each one creates and becomes the other in an eternal dance which reflects the seasons. They are mirrored in the world as action and nonaction, each one creating and begetting the other as do all opposites. We are advised to tie our action/nonaction cycles to those of the changing seasons. All human suffering, they say, comes from our attempts to resist these cyclic changes. Their prescription for avoiding diseases of stress is simple. We are told to eat when hungry and to sleep when tired.

"The superior man sets his person at rest before he moves, composes his mind before he speaks, and he makes his relationship firm before he asks for something" (*I Ching*). This is still excellent advice five thousand years after it was conceived. The advice that "The superior man does not allow his thoughts to stray beyond the immediate situation" keeps the patient from maintaining a destructive alarm state by entertaining worried thoughts about the future or angry thoughts about the past. Putting less emphasis on striving, and more on bending, Taoism teaches that it is better to lie low when the wind blows hard than to strive against the storm.

In *Harper's* magazine of November 1975, a person calling himself Peter Marin takes sharp issue with these teachings, calling them "The New Narcissism." He is concerned with " . . . the trend in therapy toward a deification of the isolated self . . . the ways in which selfishness and moral blindness now assert themselves in the larger culture as enlightenment and psychic health." The author's point of view, classically Type A, is based on the following evaluation of the human condition. "Most of us realize at one level of consciousness or another that we inhabit an age of catastrophe—if not for ourselves, then for others.'' Insofar as Peter Marin's readers believe this statement they activate their exquisitely reactive fight or flight detonator. If they read, believe, and think only this kind of thought, they go into chronic stress, experiencing *The Nameless Dreads* with all its lethal consequences. If Hans Selye's stress concept is to be accepted, we can see how an article, written out of pure compassion for a suffering humanity, can actually be a public health menace as deadly as the germs on the hands of the surgeons of Semmelweis' time.

Accurately summing up the Type B contention under attack he writes, ''They allow [people] to remain who and what they are, to accept the structured world as it is—but with a new sense of justice and justification, with the assurance that it all accords with cosmic law.''

It is exactly this change in attitude which William James calls a ''religious conversion.'' It is, indeed, the basic tenet of all humanity's great religions. Insofar as a human believes that his universe is perfect, the ''all clear'' sounds, stress abates, and health, a normal state of being, exists automatically. The body, assured that everything is O.K., turns over control to the parasympathetic nervous system which is concerned with the joys and maintenance of the physical body ... eating, sleeping, making love, and general comfort. This system shuts down immediately in response to activity of its twin complementary opposite, the sympathetic nervous system. Imagine the effect on a body which is enjoying a cup of perfectly sweetened coffee while its mind reads the following:

''Idly, for instance, we take coffee and sugar in the mornings and even that simple act immerses us immediately in the larger world. Both the coffee and the sugar have come from specific places, have been harvested by specific persons, most probably in a country where the wages paid those who do the work are exploitative and low. No doubt, too, the political system underlying the distribution of land is maintained in large part by the policies enacted and the armies acting in our name—and the reason we enjoy the coffee while others harvest it has nothing to do with indvidual will and everything to do with economics and history." Type A says, "Free suffering humanity before you think of your own comfort and joy." Type B believes that the latter is a prerequisite for the former.

A Case in Point: Dave the fence-maker has an acute case of *The Nameless Dreads*. "Somebody has pulled the plug, and this whole culture is going down the drain." He would like to go to Mexico for the summer and lay in the sun, but his protestant ethic tells him that would be a cop-out. "What would happen to the world if everyone did that?" All the time he was putting up the fence, he worried that it was somehow illegal. As a result, he saw a building inspector behind the wheel of every passing Plymouth.

"What do you think would happen if we all did only what we wanted to do? Wouldn't it all just fall apart? . . . wouldn't society simply collapse, like it did in Rome?" As we watch television pictures of Catholics killing Protestants, Christians killing Moslems, blacks killing whites, and fascists killing communists, I point out that it looks like our civilization will collapse or survive regardless of whether or not he goes to Mexico. He realizes that he can do very little to impede the imminent fall of Western civilization, but he feels impelled to try. The reason he feels impelled to try is because he sees the events taking place on the television tube as bad. A small voice inside his head is carrying an *idea* . . . "some things are good, others are evil."

This particular idea has been around since life was introduced on our planet. Judeo-Christian tradition equates the idea of good vs. evil with the ingestion of the now famous apple. When Adam bit the apple and accepted that idea, he fell from his Mexican paradise into his current worldly manifestation. As a result, Dave, the worried fence man, is afflicted with *The Nameless Dreads*. The most effective approach to a human suffering in this manner is to introduce into his consciousness the polar opposite of the infecting idea.

"Have you considered the possibility that the universe knows what it's doing, and that it means you no harm?"

"If I believed that, I'd be in Mexico for the winter and get out of this insanity."

"You don't have to believe it, you only have to consider the possibility. It's entirely possible that everything is perfect . . . We're living through the turn of the century; maybe the decay you see is merely making way for a new human renaissance. You know, when you were born, someone or something pulled a plug on you. One minute you were in a pool of warm water in a womb, the next, you were hanging upside down in some brightly lit, noisy operating room. That must have seemed like some kind of catastrophe. Many physicians think that could make you paranoid for the rest of your life." While he agrees that any trip which starts the way his did ("They held me back by pressing my mother's thighs together until her doctor arrived.") is bound to inspire mistrust and apprehension; he doesn't see how this information will help him to accept the view that the universe is perfect and that he couldn't do anything wrong even if he wanted to.

"I'd sure like to believe that, but I'd feel selfish lying out there on the beach while the world is falling about my ears." As he considers for a moment the polar opposite of his customary world view, his face lights up in a smile, and his entire body relaxes. The "all clear" has obviously been sounded . . . but only for a moment. The word "selfish" wipes the smile off his face and brings his body back to a position of military-like "AT Tension."

In order to lift this young man's depression, we must induce a change in his conscious attitude . . . a change which Dr. William James calls a religious conversion. According to the literature, the most potent agent toward this end is a vision of what is called "the living God." If he can be convinced that there is a force within him through which the universe watches over him personally, he will be cured of *The Nameless Dreads*. He will then be able to lie in the Acapulco sun and replenish his mind and body.

Lying on his back on the carpet, he is given the following instructions:

1. "Breathe deeply and slowly."

2. "As you inhale, imagine a wave of energy being pulled up the front of your body. It gets sucked into your body along with the inhaled air."

3. "As you exhale the energy pushes over the top of your head, down your back, out the back of your heels, and into the ground." (Meditators may think a mantra at this stage.)

4. "Imagine yourself in a very beautiful place, but above all keep your prime attention on the breath and the energy flow."
"I'm in a clearing in a forest. I see a pool or a lake."

5. "Look around and let me know if you see a living creature. Keep your prime attention on the breath and energy circulation."
"A fairy just flew out of the lake . . . she looks like Tinker Bell."

6. "Assume the creature is real, greet her and make friends with her. Find out her name if possible . . . ask a question, go back to your breathing and wait for an answer. If she invites your participation, imagine yourself acting accordingly. I'm going to leave you alone with her for ten minutes. Ask her about your problem . . . get her advice."

As Dave lies meditating, the phone rings. A woman says, "My seventeen-year-old son has diabetes . . . I wanted the doctor to give him Orinase because I heard it induces the pancreas to make insulin. His doctor insists on his getting insulin injections. I hate the thought of that. Do you think there is a way he could learn to make his pancreas secrete enough insulin?" She may come in for an appointment . . . meanwhile, she and her son will spend fifteen minutes a day meditating and picturing his pancreas squirting insulin into his bloodstream.

Time to see how Dave the fence man is doing.

"That was a complete mindblower!"

"What happened?"

"The fairy says her name is 'Rigor.' When I asked her what she thought about my going to Mexico, she laughed and jumped into the pool. I grabbed her by the ankle and went to the bottom with her. I was surprised that I could talk and breathe down there. When I asked her how come I feel so miserable all the time, she said 'Because you deserve it.'"

Dave further related that when he commented that the bottom of a pool was a rather trite image for the unconscious she replied, "So sue me."

Then he asked, "How come I deserve to be so miserable?"

"Because you're stupid. You think you can fix a screwed up world while you're screwed up yourself. Your prime duty is to get your own head straight. Once you've done that, then you can come back and do something effective about the state of the world."

For this patient seeing was believing. Was what he saw *real?* She is as real as your dreams; as real as this book.

At this point in our journey, it might be well to pause and inquire into the nature of such hallucinatory characters conjured up by our patients. Referring to the phenomenon of the imaginary beings such as the fairy Rigor, and the like, Carl Jung postulates the following: "Indubitably they come from the brain . . . from the inherited brain-structure itself." This is not an unreasonable concept in view of the fact that the human brain contains something in the order of thirteen and a half billion nerve cells. Compare this with a paltry one hundred thousand terminals in our modern high-speed computers.

This highly differentiated brain structure, which we inherit along with our bodies, uses only a tiny percentage of its vast circuitry to manifest and deal with our ordinary waking consciousness. The lion's share of brain structure is concerned with activities *outside* the sphere of ordinary waking awareness.

Contemporary psychiatry offers us the image of the tip of an iceberg sticking out of an infinite, timeless, black sea called "The Unconscious." The experience of I-Me (please insert your name) is today believed to be located in your left brain; specifically in a section of neural circuitry called "The Speech Center." Psychiatrists call it "The Ego."

More than thirteen and a quarter billion cells in your brain are totally unconcerned with things like the size of your bank account, your religious or national persuasion, the contents of this book, and the like. What are they about? Survival. Like "HAL," the computer in Arthur Clarke's *2001*, they monitor and maintain the human body; the spaceship used by the ego in its voyage through the infinity of time and space. Consider the effect on the I-me, you (insert your name), of this monstrously complex computer. It was operative long before you had any conscious experience of being you.

As you developed from a fertilized egg your developing brain structure experienced and recorded the history of life on the planet Earth. As you grew in your mother's womb, your brain structure experienced, monitored, and recorded the body of a single cell, like a paramecium, or a bacterium, evolving into a fish, an amphibian.

At a certain stage, the human embryo is indistinguishable from that of a salamander. The memory of having inhabited all the forms known to life on this planet was yours when you looked out from under your mother's pubic arch. It lies stored in your unconscious—the thirteen and a quarter billion nerve cells which your ego usually doesn't contemplate.

This living (bio)computer is available to you for purposes of information retrieval and guidance. You must first learn how to use it. Like "HAL," your biocomputer has a mind of its own. How does it communicate with us? Dr. Jung suggests an answer: "This unconscious, buried in the structure of the brain [discloses] its presence through creative fan-

tasy." An idea as explosive and mindblowing as $E = Mc^2$!
Dr. Jung is suggesting that the pictures we see only in our
minds, these hallucinatory nothings, are actually messages to
the tip of the iceberg from the depths of the infinite, black,
sea . . . the inherited brain structure.

"And this structure," he observes, "tells its own story
which is the story of mankind; the unending myth of death
and rebirth, and of the multitudinous figures who weave in
and out of this mystery." When a winged fairy, a butterfly
or a wise old man appeared in the mind's eye of a human
primitive, he or she did not question the experience. In those
days, the stuff which was going on inside your head when
your eyes were closed seemed just as real as the goings on inside your head when your eyes were open. Persons with vivid
dreams or active imaginations still have the same problem
today. It is my experience that many people today look at the
visions appearing behind their closed eyelids with fear and
suspicion. Fascinating! In 1976, modern human looks at the
visions inside his or her head through the eyes of our cave
dwelling forebears. We are even told today to stamp them
out in the name of mental health. Since this approach has
been so notably unsuccessful, might we not consider revers-
ing ourselves in the hope of some improvement?

The power of the visual image to totally transform life experience is a vital healing tool. It is illustrated by the case of a
young woman who was being treated at the local county
mental health clinic for about four years. She was suffering
from a severe case of *The Nameless Dreads*. Her diagnosis of
the clinic was "cancerphobia." She was convinced she had
cancer and was reacting with the appropriate amount of
anxiety, adrenaline and cortisone.

Following instructions similar to those given Dave, the
fence man, she visualized a deer who "looked like Bambi."
She asked the deer if she had cancer and the deer told her not
to be ridiculous. The word of a hallucinatory deer convinced
her where four years of skilled psychotherapy had failed.
Her attending psychiatrist contracted *The Nameless Dreads*
when he realized the implications of this particular cure.

Paracelsus states "The number of diseases that originate from some unknown cause is far greater than those that come from mechanical causes; for such diseases our physicians know no cure because not knowing such causes, they cannot remove them. All they can prudently do is observe the patient and make their guesses about his condition. The patient may rest satisfied if the medicines administered do him no serious harm and do not prevent his recovery. Unfortunately some poison their patients . . . others purge them or bleed them to death. There are some who have learned so much that their learning has driven out all their common sense, and there are others who care a great deal more for their own profit than for the health of their patients. A physician should be a servant of nature, and not her enemy. He should guide and direct her in her struggle for life and not, by unreasonable interference, throw fresh obstacles in the way of recovery."

An alchemist, Paracelsus believed that it was the function of the physician to assist his patient in the realization of his fullest and highest possible state of consciousness. Most of us think that we are merely the collection of ideas, experiences and nerve impulses which answers to a particular name (insert yours), holds a particular job, and has specific dreams, aspirations, disappointments and hopes. Paracelsus postulates that we are much more than this. We are what he called the "anthropos." The anthropos is immortal and bisexual. The particular trip in which you are currently engaged, with what you think is all your being, is only one of an infinite number of trips of which you, the anthropos, can experience . He advocates release of the "anthropos" from the chains of the material state. Essentially he was proposing the idea that human consciousness is immortal and bisexual.

Suffering and disease arise when your consciousness forgets its own immortality and starts to believe that your current life experience in the world of time and space is all there is.

Look at it from the point of view of modern astrophysics. In the course of its activities, our sun gives off enormous amounts of energy. This sun energy takes three forms: heat, light, and a flow of subatomic particles called the "solar wind." Attracted by the Earth's magnetic field, the particles incarnate themselves into our physical bodies by direct absorption through the skin at the acupuncture points or by indirect assimilation through the intake of food, air and water. Paracelsus called these carriers of celestial energy *numia*. This flow of subatomic particles, (neutrinos, pi/mesons, muons, etc.) precipitates the physical body in the course of its unceasing flux. Teilhard de Chardin maintains that the physical body consists of the entire universe. The priest-scientist (Teilhard de Chardin) and the physician (Paracelsus) both maintain that our universe is a living conscious being, consubstantial with our physical and psychic selves.

The American philosopher Alan Watts summed it up when, like a child playing hide and seek, he wrote, "You are *It*." *It*, the solar wind of subatomic particle waves streaming through our planet, has the power to excite the nerve cells in your mind (or brain, if you prefer). This excitation may be experienced as a thought, a visual image, or as an emotion. Since *It* displays isomerism (manifestation as a pair of opposites) the stream of thought, visions and feelings that courses through human existence has a light side and a dark side. The manifestations of *It* (the solar wind) may be conscious, or they may be unconscious. In any case, it seems reasonable to suggest that neural excitation by extraterrestrial forces affects human behavior and experience.

From the time of Paracelsus through the era of Freud, up to our modern day, the idea of an invisible, intangible force of nature which affects human health and behavior remains an anathema and a heresy to the scientific and medical establishment. The suggestion that this force shows intelligence is capable of driving a hard-nosed, modern scientist into an emotional crisis. In October of 1975, more than one hundred of them, astronomers, in this case, drew up a position paper in which they attacked the practitioners and followers of astrology. This idea, of cosmic forces which affect human behavior on the planet Earth in a predictable manner, was denounced as unscientific and cultist.

Insisting that talk of emanations and cosmic energy forces is taboo, they maintain that we are dealing with a universe of things, suspended out there in a place they call "space." Heads stuck in the sand of pre-Einsteinian physics, they proudly proclaim that they have even heard an echo of the "big bang"; the explosion in the primordial hydrogen-helium cloud which created our galaxy, our solar system, and us. If we ask, "Where did the hydrogen-helium cloud come from?" they tell us it was just there. Where? In "space."

What is space? Establishment astronomy tells us that space is what you have when there is no thing present. Space which contains all things is itself no thing—nothing. This nothing called space is simultaneously everywhere and nowhere. Containing all things, it is contained in every thing as the space inside the atom. Twentieth century cosmogenic explanations sound like the mystical speculations of ancient Chinese alchemists. For either to accuse the other of cultism is a case of the pot calling the kettle black. As astronomers denigrate astrology, so physicians ridicule and deny alchemy. Each scientific discipline denies its heritage and thereby cuts itself off from its roots. To do so is to wither and die.

Perhaps the difference between the theories of ancient mysticism and those of modern science are more apparent than real. Tinker Bell, a vision in the minds of James M. Barrie, Walt Disney and Dave the fence man, and many others, has been investigated by both disciplines. They agree that she is not of our time and space world. The alchemists believe she is the animating principle of matter. Clergymen speak of her as the holy spirit. Modern science may talk about her as a neural response to brain stimulation by subatomic particles. She represents "the spirit of nature." Paracelsus advises us to "guide and aid her in her struggle for life." In order to deal with the question, "Is she real?" let us examine the nature of what we call "real."

What makes a thing real to you? Many think that the fairy called "Rigor" should not be considered to be real because she could only be seen by Dave the fence man. To this point of view Sri Aurobindo, and Indian guru, responds that "The idea that an object of my perception is a hallucination if I alone perceive it, and real only if others see it as well, is an obscurantism as prejudicial to the extension of knowledge as the religious fanaticism which opposed the extension of scientific thought and discovery.''

Others think that a perception is real only if it can be touched, seen, smelled, tasted and heard. Consider the reflection of the moon on the water. Is it less real a moon than the reflecting image you can see in the heavens? The image in the sky, they maintain, is the true moon. A shaky assumption at best since one can neither touch, taste, feel or hear either visual image. We decide arbitrarily between experiences and perceptions which are real and those which are not. These decisions, based as they are on current *ideas* regarding the nature of reality, radically affect our life on the planet.

Current ideas regarding visual images inside your head which only you can see differ sharply from those held by Paracelsus who wrote: "There is an earthly sun, which is the cause of all heat, and all who are able to see may see the sun; and those who are blind may feel his heat. There is an eternal sun, which is the source of all wisdom, and those whose spiritual senses have awakened to life will see that sun and be conscious of his existence; but those who have not attained spiritual consciousness may yet feel his power by an inner faculty which is called intuition.''

The power of the visual image to perform religious conversions and thereby totally transform life experience is compatible with the suggestion that it is that visual image which we call the holy ghost. It is possible that the image we see in our minds is actually the spiritual sun which appears to us in order to guide and assist our evolution in the realm of time and space. In order to taste of the Type B state of grace, we need merely to concede that Paracelsus *might* be right. We need only to explore the kingdom within, without prejudgment, and evaluate the effects of these explorations on our daily mundane existence.

How, you may ask, can looking at the pictures inside my head affect the real world out there? Lillian, one young woman who came to our clinic, became furious when I suggested that she ask the figures in her mind what they could tell her about the reasons for her recurrent bladder infections. "My infection is not in my mind," she snapped. "It's in my damn bladder!" Insisting that the change had to occur in some objective extrapersonal real world rather than merely in her experience, she dismissed as ritual any therapeutic procedure which did not directly affect the germs in her bladder. Her attitude was that of the wife who closed the window in response to her husband's suggestion that it was cold outside and said, "Now I suppose it's warmer outside?"

Consider the example of the paleolithic cave drawings which by their representation of the animal being slain by the hunter are supposed to increase his prowess and bring success in the hunt. In his *Origins and History of Consciousness*, psychologist Erich Neumann writes: "We can establish as a scientific fact that the rite is not likely to have any objective effect upon the animal; but that is not to say that the magic rite is therefore illusion, infantile and mere wishful thinking. The magical effect of the rite is factual enough, and in no sense illusory. Moreover, it actually works out, just as primitive man supposes, in his hunting successes; only the effect does not proceed via the object, but via the subject."

Just as changing the attitude of the hunter enhances and alters his ability to perform, so changes in the attitude of the patient enhance the body's healing powers. "In both cases," Dr. Neumann continues, "our enlightened rationalism misunderstands the magic prayer (and meditation) as illusory, in its scientific pride at having established that the object cannot be influenced. In both cases it is wrong. An effect that proceeds from an alteration in the subject is objective and real."

An important way in which we can influence our subjects to switch from a pathogenic (disease producing) Type A world view is to ask them to reconsider their attitude toward death. We are taught that inevitable and inexorable death waits in the wings ready to snuff out our pitifully small existence, mocking at all our efforts to give any meaning at all to life. Life (consciousness) is said to be a tiny flash of light placed between two infinite and eternal blacknesses. Compare the alchemical doctrine of the "anthropos," which postulates the immortality of your own awareness. Remember, all you have to do to sound the "all clear" and banish *The Nameless Dreads* is to consider the possibility that the following suggestion just *might* be true. There are those who claim that the universe, as a living conscious intelligence, descends into the illusion of material existence for a brief period of time. M. P. Hall in his encyclopedia on ancient religious beliefs describes the *Anthropos* as " . . . that which never clothes itself in the sheath of matter."

In terms of personal experience, the anthropos would be that part of your mind, the deepest and most inside part, which can watch the goings on and remark "I can't believe this is happening to me." In the middle of a furious argument, it can suddenly dissociate itself from the ongoing frenzy and silently ponder, "I wonder why I'm doing this?" It is the part of your consciousness, the very central part, which, as the years go by, looks at its perpetually changing reflection in the mirror and exclaims, "That can't really be me in that mirror!" At death, according to this ancient theory, this part of you wakes up as if from a dream and says something like: "Far out, what a great trip that was, I think I'll try it again." Imagine the therapeutic effect of this idea in the case of one who sees the death of a loved one as a source of excruciating pain and anguish, and who contemplates personal death with abject terror. Since we can't possibly know for certain about any of it, we might as well adopt attitudes toward life, death and the universe which do not damage and destroy our physical bodies.

Is there any evidence to suggest that the doctrine of the reincarnating anthropos may indeed have some foundation in fact? In a discussion of this sort, people often make an emotional decision and categorically state that they don't (or do) believe in reincarnation and immortality of something called the soul. The scientific method requires that we merely collect the data and evaluate it without prejudice. At the beginning, we must presume that either of the two opposing positions are equally possible. In his *Crack in the Cosmic Egg*, J. C. Pierce states: "In a continuum of possibilities any possibility is equally valid." This means that in a situation where no one is certain exactly what is going on, anybody's theory is as valid as anyone else's. It is, of course, possible to embrace either point of view on pure faith and intuition, but this is not to be considered a scientific approach.

At this point in our discussion, it might be a good idea to illustrate some of the ideas we have been considering with clinical case material in order to demonstrate their exquisite relevance to the practice of healing sick people. Lillian, who insisted that her infection was in her bladder and not in her mind, stated that she had had a burning sensation in her pelvis for the past twelve years. Her vagina was constantly sore, painful and inflamed, and every time she passed urine she experienced a distressingly severe burning sensation. Her diagnosis, made after several careful physical and laboratory investigations, was *nonspecific vaginitis, nonspecific urethritis* and *chronic cystitis*. Her kidney Xray, called a pyelogram, showed normal kidney structure and function.

This case is particularly interesting, because at this moment, there are approximately eleven million Americans suffering from nonspecific or resistant infections of the bladder and its exit conduit, the urethra. The term nonspecific means that her examining physicians have no notion regarding the cause of her genitourinary inflammation.

As Paracelsus pointed out, this is one of the majority of diseases which originate from an unknown cause. He says that all we can do is "observe the patient and make guesses about his (her) condition." Hippocrates warned us: "Above all do not make the patient worse." Sir William Osler reminded us that: "It is more important to know the patient who has the disease than to know the disease which has the patient."

Since she was unwilling to talk to figures in her own mind, Lillian was asked to lie down and circulate her energy in the same manner as Dave the fence man. She agreed to imagine that the energy was a stream of cool water which circulated through her fiery pelvis and ran out to the sea. After ten minutes of this, a vibrating tuning fork was applied to several acupuncture points on her body.

"How are you feeling now?" I asked.

"My pelvis feels better, the burning is smaller in area, but now it feels as if there is a clot of knotted ropes inside my lower parts." She also reported that her lower back felt as if there was a block of cement imbedded in the muscles. She spent the next ten minutes visualizing the ropes being untied and smoothed out, and the cement block being dissolved by the stream of circulating water-energy. At the end of the thirty-minute treatment, she reported that the symptom was thirty percent improved. "It burns just as bad, but it seems to cover a much smaller area. That's the first time in twelve years that I've gotten any sort of relief!"

Recall the words of Erich Neumann: "Any effect that proceeds from an alteration in the subject is objective and real." She was advised to spend twenty minutes daily for the next week lying quietly, breathing, circulating cold-water energy through her pelvis, untying and smoothing the knotted ropes, and dissolving the cement block in her lower back. Encouraged by her success, she agreed. One week later she was back asking, "Do you believe in reincarnation? I mean past lives and stuff like that." She then recounted an experience which her friends had received with amazement and disbelief. "If it hadn't happened to me, I wouldn't believe it either . . . Last Sunday night, I was doing my imagery and breathing, when I felt myself going into some sort of deep trance . . . Is it possible to hypnotize yourself?" When I told her that it was indeed possible, she seemed greatly relieved. "It must have been a hypnotic trance . . . Anyway, I saw this coyote . . . the name 'Wildwood' flashed into my mind when I saw him . . . Then, he just started talking to me!"

"What did he say?"

"He said to pay attention to what happened, and not to worry as he would stay close by my side through the whole experience."

"What happened then?"

"The room disappeared and I became unaware of time and space. Then I saw a light which gradually got brighter and started to flicker. I suddenly realized that I was an Indian woman in a black dress seated in front of a campfire. I had a vision of a group of male Indians dancing around the fire. As I watched them I became aware that I was bound. I realized that I must have been a captive in the hands of an enemy tribe. I actually experienced being gang raped and murdered. As I died, I saw myself in a field of pure red which gradually turned into my room and I awoke." As she spoke tears streamed down her cheeks. "The coyote was by my side the whole time, reassuring and comforting me."

Is Lillian a reincarnated Mohawk Indian maiden whose pelvis burns because of something that happened in a previous lifetime? Did she assemble facts and bits of information gleaned from her reading, movie and TV watching and concoct a meaningless fantasy? Is she an overwrought chronically ill female on the verge of a nervous breakdown? There are many possible explanations. Within this continuum of possibilities, all are equally valid. Your explanation is as valid as any other. Just don't fall into the trap of thinking you know how it really is.

Is there really such a phenomenon as reincarnation? Well, it all depends on your point of view. Look at it this way. Suppose we substitute the concept of incarnation of molecules of desoxyribonucleic acid in place of the alchemical "reincarnating anthropos." DNA is the stuff in the genes which, like the anthropos, is immortal but creates for itself a vehicle of flesh so that it can become you in a physical body. Are the geneticists and the alchemists describing the same phenomenon in different terms? Is consciousness immortal? By consciousness, I am referring to that state of *empty awareness* you experience when you rouse from a deep sleep suddenly. I am referring to that moment when you are aware of being awake, but are not certain of who or where you are. You are not actually aware of the existence of your physical body until someone asks you. "How do you feel today?"

Dr. Elizabeth Kubler-Ross, an American research psychiatrist, has reported her research with dying patients and those who were temporarily dead, but brought back by modern medical technology. She feels that her data supports the working hypothesis that human consciousness persists beyond the state we today call physical death. Our machines have brought people back from the state we still call legally dead: no heartbeat, no respiration, fixed, staring eyes with slowly dilating pupils which do not respond to light. People who have been brought back from this state report that they were aware of some sort of continued existence outside the dead physical body. Faced, as we are with data of this nature, we have to revise drastically our current notions regarding death as a medical entity, consciousness as a living entity, or both. We will have to content ourselves at this point with the observation that anything is possible since nothing has been proven (according to the requirements of the scientific method). Consciousness may or may not continue after death. No one really *knows* for sure unless they themselves have had such an experience. Then, of course, they don't care what anyone else thinks.

People can have the experience of existence outside the physical body without the intervention of the state we call death. Lillian's experience is a case in point. An interesting theory is the view of a gentlemen named David under treatment at about the same time. David is an elderly gentlemen who looks like God. Full, white hair, and a flowing white beard, surrounding a strong, alert, age-lined face. He has written a poem which describes his work:

"As the dream unrolls on the screen of the mind
as the mind travels through vast worlds
whirling in the imagining eye,
the dreamer asks and is asked;
Who is the dancer leaping across the far star shores of
consciousness?
Who is the artist watching the picture emerge on the
canvas of the dream?"

The poem is part of the brochure advertising workshops
which he calls "Dreaming in a magical playhouse . . . Playing in a magical dream." The goal of the workshop sessions
is stated as follows in the brochure:

>   "Self realized by the self
>   who knows It is playing
>   all the roles
>   in
>   this magical dream
>   It is dreaming.

Essentially he is postulating the hypothesis that we are making up our entire life experience. We make it up as we go
along, so to speak. He is suggesting along with Erich
Neumann that *as your consciousness evolves and grows
stronger, it becomes able to control and direct its own life experience.*

>   "Awareness awakens
>   The eternal player perceives who is
>   playing
>   the eternal game."

Life, Death and Awareness

The state of being which we call death is characterized legally by an absence of electrical activity in the formerly living brain. Our definition has become more refined as our diagnostic tools have grown in sophistication. Early physicians made the dread diagnosis on the basis of their trained sense organs. The patient was considered dead if the doctor could not detect a heartbeat, and if a pulse was not palpable at the wrists. The limitations of this method were emphasized by Groucho Marx when he grabbed his friend's wrist, looked at his timepiece and gravely announced, "Either this man is dead or my watch has stopped." Technology came to the aid of the hunt for the smallest spark of what we call life, when a mirror was first held to the nose and lips of the corpse in the hope that it would reveal persistent breathing by turning cloudy. The electrocardiograph amplified our senses of touch and hearing by detecting persistent electrical activity in the cardiac conduction system. (This is the system which stimulates the heart muscle to contract.) The spur for all the refinements in detection of miniscule life processes may well have been man's primal fear of being buried alive. Absence of breath and heart activity when accompanied by dilated, unresponsive pupils was considered final evidence of death as late as 1971. By 1975, it was decided that a person was dead when his electroencephalogram (EEG) was flat. This indicates cessation of electrical activity in the brain. Today, a functioning heart may be removed from a body which demonstrates a flat EEG tracing. The essential center of our existence has been raised from the heart, which is considered the seat of the soul, to the brain, which we believe to be the container of the mind.

What about the subjective experience of dying? One is tempted to speculate on how it interacts with the mind. Ancient writings like the *Tibetan Book of the Dead* presume that the mind continues to function after it has left the realm of time and space. Consider the experience of a man named Sollo. He was driving home from a movie with his wife sitting beside him, and stopped for a red light. Turning to his wife, he spoke her name and slumped over the wheel. A passing policeman administered cardiac massage and mouth-to-mouth resuscitation while his partner radioed for an ambulance, which responded immediately. Mr. Sollo was then transferred to a nearby hospital and placed in intensive care. His heart and breathing had been stopped for twenty-eight minutes. Thanks to modern medical technology, his brain oxygen supply was kept at adequate levels until his vital functions resumed spontaneously. When I first saw him, or to be more precise, when I first saw his image, he was describing what it felt like to be dead. "I was in an energy field. When your body and its senses stop, you leave one world and enter another. I felt like I was on a sort of a journey. There was nothing painful or anxiety producing on that other plane. I did not know where I was going, but since coming back, I have completely lost my fear of death. I would advise everyone in that situation to just relax and accept the inevitable."

The morning paper carries the story of Mr. Faulk, a forty-four-year-old tennis playing weight lifter who, like Mr. Sollo, was brought back from the dead. Keep in mind, both these patients were dead according to the standard of definition of death prevailing in American hospitals at that time. Mr. Faulk, the paper said, had been stabbed in the chest while walking with his wife in the park. "The couple said they had gone to the park because they considered the beach unsafe. A passerby called for an ambulance which sped the victim to the Hospital Medical Center about five miles away. Paramedics administered oxygen and fluids enroute, the surgeon was summoned to be ready. He went right to work. There was no time to wait for the anesthetic. There was no pulse or blood pressure . . . the man was essentially dead at the time. The heart specialist made an incision in the chest, spread the ribs, and stitched up the punctured heart. Despite the absence of anesthetic, the patient lapsed into unconsciousness and could feel no pain even though he thrashed about wildly. He was listed in stable condition and was expected to live, the hospital said.''

The NBC Nightly News, the same day, carried the same story. The victim had recovered sufficiently to describe the incident from a different point of view, his mind locating itself in infinite space somewhere inside the skull of the stabbed and sutured body of a man named Faulk. "It all happened so fast . . . there were these three guys . . . they pushed me down and I felt blood on my hand . . . it was from my chest. I knew I had been stabbed. Then everything went grey and it all sort of faded out. I don't remember a thing about the operation.''

To the mind calling itself Mr. Sollo, time and space faded out. To the mind of Mrs. Sollo time and space remained constant, while Mr. Sollo faded out. To the mind of Mr. Faulk, everything faded out. Who, then, was thrashing his body around during the operation? What is the exact location in space of the "energy field" described by Mr. Sollo and by the authors of the *Tibetan Book of the Dead*? As you read these words, *can you locate the space which contains your own mind, and can you exactly locate the boundaries of that space?*

Most of us think of space as unlimited nothingness. Nothingness called outer space is known to be black. Inside-the-mind nothingness is called death if it is permanent, and unconsciousness or syncope if it is transient. The states of death and depression are also said to be subjectively black, as is deep dreamless sleep. The delta state, or sleep, is characterized on the EEG by a condition in which the needles of the machine move fewer than four times per second. Most Western Earth people consider delta the only permissible incursion into inside-the-mind nothingness. Many even resent the need for it, claiming; "When you're sleeping, you're not living." They fear all other subjectively black states of mind, and they are positively terrified at the thought of death; permanent black nothingness. The extent of this terror was made evident by the thrashings of the body of Mr. Faulk. It took eight men to hold it down while his mind rested peacefully in the blackness of a death-like coma. Our other explorer of the other shore, the mind of Mr. Sollo, left its body lying inert and lifeless as it actively examined its new surroundings. The former mind experienced *nothing*, while the latter experienced *something*. The former was *off*, the latter was *on*.

A colleague, Marty the medical director, recounted a pertinent experience which occurred while he was on duty in the emergency room—an experience which he feels is crucial.

"I was finishing up a sixteen hour shift; it was eleven p.m. after a completely insane day. I tell you, if I thought it was real, I wouldn't have been able to handle it. I had two cardiac arrests and a bad auto accident, while the waiting room was jammed with people with the flu. My shift was over and I was on my way out when they wheel this guy right by me. He'd ODed on heroin. He wasn't breathing, and his face was dark blue. There wasn't anyone else around, so I shoved a tube down his windpipe and pumped some oxygen into his lungs. That pinked him up a good bit. Then I gave him a shot of this new opiate antagonist. It's like Nalline only it wakes 'em right up, like turning on a switch. One minute this guy is laying there, blue, his head hanging off the back of the table, mouth open, tongue hanging out; by the time I get the needle out of the vein, he's cursing, screaming, vomiting blood, and trying to kill everyone in sight, primarily me. There are nine of us holding him down, while he vomits all over me trying to get a strangle hold on my neck yelling, 'I'll kill you, you mother! Why don't you mind your own fucking business and leave me alone!'

"In the midst of all this, my mind suddenly became very peaceful and still. I was somewhere in the back of my head watching my body continue to act out the scene as it fought a madman for survival. The thought then struck me that both of us were in exactly the same situation. I began to get a clear picture of what had happened in his mind. I pictured a guy going through the hassle of scoring some heroin, getting himself real comfortable and safe, and shooting it into his vein. Everything started to turn grey and slowly faded out until it was all black. The whole flash happened in a fraction of an instant. I realized what it must feel like to have that blackness suddenly switch into a body with a tube in the windpipe, tubes in both arms, and a mouth full of blood and vomit. At that instant I was back in my body fighting for my life (as was my patient).

"I started thinking about this business of snatching people back from the dead even against their obvious and violent opposition. We seem to think we have some God-given commandment to do this. I feel like that, but I'm not sure it makes any sense."

He knows he will give that incident a great deal of thought because "I'm sure it had a heavy message for me."

The descriptions brought back by persons presumed dead correspond to the states of existence and nonexistence postulated by Earth's Eastern religions. The on and off states of the mind correspond to the contracted and relaxed states of the heart. The mind, like the heart, must alternate between the polar opposites in order to perform its function. This undulation between on and off, systole and diastole, is a basic characteristic of all we know. The twin snakes on the caduceus, symbol of the healing arts, embody this upward spiraling motion. The wriggling of the snake illustrates the path of a subatomic particle in a cloud chamber, the double spiral of the DNA molecule (the memory bank which contains the complete record of the experience of life as matter on the Earth), the path of our solar system in a rotating spiral galaxy, and anything else you could possibly think of. Everything, on every level conceivable to the mind, is wriggling. Wriggling is what is meant by serpent power, and wriggling is what is meant by wave action. At the turn of the twentieth century, we know that electricity is some kind of mysterious wriggling which can be carried in wires to plugs in walls where it lights bulbs and makes all kinds of machines do incredible things. We know what it does—we don't know what it is.

The word, energy can be used instead of wriggling, but the latter is much more precise. Albert Einstein taught that *things* are not different from wriggles. The one is convertible into the other by means of the formula $E = MC^2$. The formula translates as: "lumps moving at the speed of light are pure wriggles." Einstein repeats the ideas of Christ ("I am the light") . . . when he tells us that light is at the boundary between matter and vibration (spirit).

It is light which carries a pattern of wriggles to my retina, forming the intermediary between my mind (whose boundaries I have yet to define) and *things* in space. All our senses translate wriggle patterns in space to wriggle patterns in the mind. We can only experience the pattern of energy making the *thing out there* indirectly after it has been carried like a baton in a relay race through the environment to the senses, through the nervous system, to the brain into the mind. *We experience the wriggle, not the thing.*

Wriggling, as symbolized by the caduceus, is an autonomous activity. It is visualized by twentieth century scientific and popular thought as something which is done by things. (Things make wriggles, or things wriggle.) The Einsteinian concept of $E = MC^2$ which asserts that things can *become* wriggles has not yet filtered down into the mass consciousness of the West. The dominant consciousness in this part of the planet has yet to catch on to Immanuel Kant's suggestion that the thing itself, the objective *thing* "out there" which is initiating the wriggles, is forever and completely unknowable to the mind.

Turn of the century consciousness is aware of the fact that light itself is neither a wriggle nor a thing, yet it is somehow both. The bridge is established by the theory of complementarity which states that the behavior of light is explainable only by the assumption that it exists in two mutually exclusive forms . . . particle and wave. It acts like one when it doesn't happen to be acting like the other.

The Soviet scientist V. Inyushin has formalized a theory which reverses Descartes' dualism of wriggling and things. He suggests that "wriggles" also *thing*. The theory of bioplasmic energy suggests that the entire universe known to the mind is composed of vibrations. Finer vibratory rates (very fast wriggles) are perceived by the mind as thought. When the vibrations in the mind get coarse and alter their pattern, the mind creates the impression of things out there in space. An analogy would be a blur which speeds into our view and stops, revealing itself as some thing (a car, an insect, or whatever). The mediator which converts vibrations into objects in time and space is the image making power of the mind. The objective time/space world out there, the dreamy subjective world of fantasy, dreams, hallucinations and ecstatic visions, as well as the intermediate experience of inhabiting a physical body, are examples of the ability of the mind to convert wriggles into patterns we call images. It seems reasonable to postulate that "in here" (mind pictures),"out there" (the real world) and the body in between are all contained within the mind. You can't fix the limit of your mind in space, because space is a product of the mind rather than vice versa as some of us have been led to believe.

The practical aspect of all this lies in the idea that by altering its rate of vibration, the mind can alter the state of the physical matter constituting its environment. The sciences which concern themselves with the interaction between things and wriggles are called "psychotronics" and "physics." The former examines how mental vibrations crystallize as things. The ability of the mind to affect the matter contained within the space occupied by the body has enormous implications for the healing arts. The ancient symbol for these arts, the caduceus, is, among other things, a tribute to "wriggle power."

The Clash of the Paradigms

A paradigm is a view of the world which is accepted as absolutely true beyond any shadow of doubt. It differs from a religion in that it is not supposed to be accepted as a matter of blind faith. Before a theory can be accepted as axiomatic, or always true, it must pass the test of scrutiny by means of the scientific method. A typical paradigm clash surfaced in the California public school system in 1974.

At issue was the question of what to tell the kids about how it all got started. *What are the origins of the world around us? How did it get to be like it is today?* One group, the Cartesian scientific materialists, insisted that only *their* theory be presented in textbooks. They believe that the world got to be like we see it today through a process of evolution. It all started, they say, with a "big bang" or primeval explosion in space (out there in black nothingness). Our galaxy, our solar system and our planet are just lumps of debris which have been set whirling and spinning by the original explosion. Rocks, trees, living creatures, and the body we inhabit are random collections of this debris which just happened to arrange itself in a manner which made it able to live, reproduce, and finally think. The mind, that which makes me uniquely me, is supposed to be nothing but a series of electrical discharges in the inert matter constituting the brain.

Opposing them were the Judeo-Christians who believe that the world was created from nothing in six days by a mind which they call God. The mind of man is said to be a reflection of the original mind of God which brought everything we know into being. The physical universe, or, as they call it, manifestation, is merely a thought in the mind of God. Twentieth century conventional wisdom referred to these points of view as the *theory* of evolution vs. the *myth* of creation. Notice that one is called a theory while the other is called a myth.

The California Supreme Court, in a landmark decision, decided that neither side had proven its case conclusively under the rules of evidence. Textbooks on science in California schools are today required to present both theories impartially. Each group still clings to its own opinion, accusing the other of ignorance and heresy. School children, preparing to live in the twenty-first century, have the opportunity to examine both points of view, and to make up their own minds.

Cartesian healers ply their trade by attempting to rearrange inert lumps of matter. Religious healers appeal to the mind of God to intervene and correct the misbehavior of His creation. The mind of the patient places its body in the hands of one or the other and hopes for the best. All cling to the opinion that healing originates outside; in the form of a prescription from the physician or a dispensation from the Lord.

The proponents of the myth of creation won their last major battle in the nineteenth century when they busted a high school teacher for teaching the theory of evolution. In the now famous Scopes Monkey Trial, the decision was rendered in their favor. The issue and conflict swirling around a simple lesson plan: *"What are the origins of the world around us, and how did it get to be like it is?"* remains unresolved. All we can say for sure is that there are two opposing views, and there is conflict between them.

Suppose we presume them both to be equally true, as we are required to do according to the "law of complementarity" (see Arthur Koestler; *Roots of Coincidence*). We would have to tell the kids that the world was created just the way it is, by a mind which was there before the world was. The world is constantly evolving and changing, we would say (in deference to Darwin's famous theory). As a physician I would be required, by this fusion of opposite theories, to completely change a basic assumption of twentieth century medical practice. I have always supposed that the body creates the mind. Now I must enlarge my view and allow that the mind creates the body, just the way it is now. With a nod to Charles Darwin, I would presume that both are constantly changing their state. Mind and body are in a state of perpetual evolutionary transformation . . . a constant becoming. I could presume a state of continuous creation in which the wriggle patterns in the mind (which we perceive as thought) "thing," or *crystallize* in space as the tissues and organs of my patient's body.

The hypothesis that the world is a biohologram projected by the mind through thought is ancient and venerable. Taoism and Tibetan Buddhism, among other Eastern paradigms, maintain that the illusory body of the patient exists only in the mind. For purposes of our discussion let us assume we mean the mind of the patient who brings his body in for repair. Most of my intelligent, sophisticated patients were under the impression that medical research has discovered something in the brain which proves that in the place where the mind is supposed to be, there is only matter. Most of my intelligent, sophisticated colleagues believe to this date that in the space where the body organs are supposed to be, there is only matter. Contrast that with the Eastern paradigm "there is only mind," and you have a pair of opposites.

The theory of complementarity is really a basic alchemical formula transposed into contemporary terminology. The fusion of the opposites (the mystical marriage) is said to result in their annihilation. The result of their union is a third entity which is at the same time both its parents and neither. The symbol for the fused, higher entity is the child. The child symbol in alchemy is an obvious allusion to the biologic process of reproduction. The entire field of chemistry is built on the alchemical instructions to "dissolve and fuse." Sodium Chloride (table salt) is neither positively ionized sodium, nor is it a negative ion floating around in a cloud of poisonous chlorine gas. It is the offspring of a heiros gamos (mystical marriage) of the two which annihilated its parents and created table salt as new taste thrill.

The particle physicists tell us that if a positron collides with its opposite, an electron, the two annihilate each other in a flash emitting two photons (packets of wriggles which the mind perceives as light). If the heiros gamos sheds light on the experiments of the physicists, why shouldn't it do the same for the physicians?

THE MARRIAGE OF THE PARADIGMS

In a statement which makes me suspect that yesterday's alchemists are today's nuclear scientists, quantum physicist Wolfgang Pauli tells us, "It would be a more satisfactory solution if mind and body could be interpreted as complementary aspects of the same reality." The mind creates the body and the body creates the mind. Mind and body relate to each other as two mirrors facing; each reflecting and creating the other. We can postulate that they are complementary aspects of a single reality. *Mind and body, we may theorize, are two faces of a single other entity which is characterized by constant and continuous change (evolution).* This entity is *awareness.* The question of how or when constant and continuous change got started can be left to the philosophers. The physician must deal with a patient in the here and now who wants relief of suffering and not a history lesson. In the consultation room, I am faced with a mind/body which is saying "fix my body" or "fix my mind." Under the rules of our new paradigm, we would consider that we are dealing with an evolving mind/body signaling distress.

Cookbook Alchemy was the basis of the last part of the clinical experiment at the Headlands Health Service, the demise of which we will discuss in Chapter V. However, the procedure was to first dissolve our evolving mind/matter/patient into a pair of opposites. The mind is assigned the role of the alchemical King Sol (the sun). This aspect of our warring duality is arbitrarily considered male or positive. The body plays the role of Queen Luna (the moon). She is considered female, and resides at the negative pole of our duality. The King (mind) and Queen (body) are placed in a tub of water. We presume this to mean that the mind and the body are to stop all usual activities and face each other in a relaxed state . . . like lovers in a bath. People need to be reminded that your mind and your body are part of a single unity—that unity is you (please insert your name). This is accomplished by meditating, reciting a mantra, and deep regular breathing, among other means. At the clinic, we administered energy in the form of a beam of high frequency wriggles of a quartz crystal. This beam directed into the acupuncture system produced the requisite state of mind and body relaxation.

The alchemical heiros games (mystical marriage) requires that the King and Queen have intercourse under the surface of the water. Dr. Carl Jung suggests that the water represents the unconscious. For the purpose of our experiment, let us presume the water to mean the space described by Mr. Sollo . . . a field of pure energy. The mind and the body of the patient are to have some sort of intercourse in the watery underworld. The attitude of the civilized Western mind toward entering into *inside black nothingness* (unconsciousness) is exemplified by the thrashings around of Mr. Faulk's body . . . an attitude of abject terror. Many Western urban earthlings have difficulty entering delta (falling asleep). Others are afraid of out there blackness (the dark). Ultrasound acupuncture helps us relax the mind of the patient (King) from its cramp of consciousness. This is the state experienced by the mind of Mrs. Sollo when she saw her husband turn blue and slump over after he called her name.

The mind of Mr. Sollo had entered a state which was neither out-there-time-space, nor inside-black-nothing. "I was in an energy field. When your body and its senses stop, you leave one world and enter another." We suggest to the mind of the patient that it enter into this other world of pure energy. The mind of the patient stays in touch with the world of time/space by talking with the doctor or healer. The doctor tells the patient to imagine the energy or light in the field circulating up the front of the body as it breathes in and moving down the back with exhalation. (Unlike that of Mr. Sollo, our patients' bodies were able to breathe on their own.) The energy seems to advance and recede like an ocean wave . . . this gives the image of immersion to the mind and body under treatment.

This trick of the mind, its ability to switch off time/space reality and substitute an energy field, is the single most powerful healing tool available to humanity. (This area is more completely explored in *The Healing Mind.*) Alchemy's mystical marriage keeps its promise and produces "the panacea which cures all ills." The results of this phase of the experiment were published under the title "Acupuncture with High Frequency Sound—A preliminary report."

Reprint from
The Osteopathic Physician

ACUPUNCTURE WITH HIGH FREQUENCY SOUND

The Headlands clinic was first founded in 1971 as a project of the Presbyterian Synod of the Golden Gate. Our purpose has been to find ways of improving the delivery of health care, using as a target a California town of about two thousand population. Our concern has been the development of improved techniques which would be valid for the problems faced by the general medical practitioner. The therapeutic modalities which we have evaluated include allopathic medicine; OMT; alpha wave biofeedback; meditation; mental imagery during a light, autogenically induced trance state; milieu therapy; and, most recently, sonopuncture—which is a variant of acupuncture using ultrasound stimulation instead of needles.

Our purpose in this report is to describe our preliminary

observations in the last named procedure. Alpha wave bio-feedback was reported in *Medical World News*, March 9, 1973. The "Physiology of Meditation" was reported in *Scientific American*, February 1972. Biofeedback is being used currently to restore motion to paralyzed limbs, to lower blood pressure, and to control heart rate. This work is described in *Physician's World*, June 1973.

Carl Simonton, M.D., of the American Cancer Society, has been working at Travis Air Force Base in California (David Grant Medical Center). He is reporting cures of far advanced malignancies using visualization techniques. He now has a grant to pursue this therapeutic modality, and should be reporting his results soon. We have observed significant results on a general practice level with this procedure as well. There is an allusion to the technique in *The Well Body Book* (Random House 1973) by M. Samuels, M.D., a member of our staff.

In July 1972 the author participated in a conference held in Moscow between U.S. and Russian scientists. One of the participants was Dr. V. M. Inyushin, a renowned physicist in the U.S.S.R. In the course of his paper on bioenergetics and its practical applications, he made reference to work in progress at the Medical Center of Kazakh State University, where he heads the Department of Physics. They are directing low-intensity laser radiation into the acupuncture points of patients with bone malignancies. Their preliminary work shows reversal of the tumor growth, and subsequent regeneration of destroyed bone tissue.

Other subjects covered at this conference were reported in *The Osteopathic Physician*, October 1972. An excellent description of the current state of U.S.-U.S.S.R. cooperation in the field of bioenergetics can be found in *Galaxies of Life* (Interface 1973) edited by Stanley Krippner, Ph.D.

On the basis of this rapidly unfolding series of concepts, we decided to do a clinical study using ultrasound instead of laser radiation, since the former is a modality with which Dr. Oyle has had wide experience in his 15 years of general practice.

To date we have treated 33 patients with sonopuncture as the exclusive modality. The machine we are using is a Sonicator ultrasonic therapy unit. The output from the head is 1 megacycle from a 5 cm² crystal. The dosage we have been using is 0.6 watts per square centimeter for three minutes. The energy output from the Sonicator head is directed into the acupuncture points, using the therapeutic sites suggested by Dr. Felix Mann of Cambridge, England. There are many courses and references now available for the physician interested in learning about the anatomical distribution of the acupuncture meridians and points.

Our patient sample consists of 33 consecutive patients who came to our office following our decision to initiate the study. Patients presenting complaints included acute low back pain, joint pain following finger dislocation (previously reduced elsewhere), dysuria with fever, second degree burn of forearm with cellulitis, allergic dermatitis, dysmenorrhea, severe tooth pain, and acute anxiety reactions.

Sonopuncture (clinical data)

Signs & symptoms	Age & Sex		Response*
Blunt trauma (eyebrow)	24	M	Good
Low back pain	27	F	Excellent
Shoulder girdle pain	29	M	Excellent
Shoulder girdle pain	47	M	Excellent
Shoulder girdle pain	26	F	Good
Second degree burn (forearm)	31	M	Excellent
Acute anxiety reaction	21	M	Excellent
Acute anxiety reaction	33	M	Excellent
Allergic dermatitis	31	M	Excellent
Acute anxiety reaction	31	F	Good
Upper back pain	29	F	Fair
Upper back pain	26	F	Excellent
Acute anxiety reaction	22	M	Good

Traumatic arthritis (middle phalange joint)	26	M	Good
Sty	26	F	Good
Low back pain	21	M	Good
Acute anxiety reaction	50	F	Good
Abscess	28	M	Good
Acute anxiety reaction	20	M	Excellent
Traumatic arthritis (wrist)	21	M	Poor
Neck pain	26	F	Excellent
Low back pain	44	F	Poor
Paraplegic post/op low back pain	36	F	Excellent
Toothache (caries)	26	M	Excellent
Blunt trauma (forehead)	38	F	Poor
Shoulder pain (traumatic)	23	M	Fair
Low back pain	31	M	Excellent
Dysmenorrhea	33	F	Excellent
Low back pain	24	M	Excellent
Asthmatic wheezing	8	M	Excellent
Blunt trauma (thumb)	30	M	Poor
Traumatic arthritis (elbow)	41	M	Excellent
Acute anxiety reaction	35	F	Excellent

*Response scale:

Excellent—75 to 100% resolution of symptoms in 24 hours

Good   —50 to 75% resolution to symptoms in 24 hours

Fair   —25 to 50% resolution of symptoms in 24 hours

Poor   — 0 to 25% resolution of symptoms in 24 hours

Our observed results have been truly remarkable. Each patient demonstrated marked clinical improvement within 24 hours, some within 30 minutes after treatment. In addition, there was a marked sedative or tranquilizing effect, lasting in some cases for several days. One patient compared the effect to "taking three reds" (Seconal); another claimed the treatment was "better than one hour of meditation"; a third felt "as if I had just taken ½ grain of phenobarbital." Other

comments included "I feel so relaxed, I can't talk" . . .
"Layers of energy are being unwrapped." Five patients
noted increased clarity of vision and intensified color perception.

In order to come up with a viable explanation for these
and other findings with acupuncture therapy, we must postulate a fourth circulatory system. The other three with which
we are familiar are the cardiovascular, the lymphatic and the
cerebrospinal systems. The fourth system postulated by the
ancient Chinese and modern day physicists (see *Galaxies of
Life*) is pure electromagnetic energy carried in currents along
meridians, or paths. Our physical bodies can be conceived of
as patterned arrangements of electrolyte solutions whose
laminar flow produces electromagnetic fields probably relat-
ing to the acupuncture meridian system. This electromagnetic energy is called "Chi" by the Chinese and "bioplasmic
energy" by the Russian physicists. Manipulation of this
energy by needles, massage, OMT, heat, laser light, or high
frequency sound is a therapeutic modality which far surpasses any other approach we have used in two years of
operation of our clinic.

We have conducted a preliminary clinical study of 33 patients using ultrasound to effect standard acupuncture treatment in illnesses including low back pain, second degree
burn, allergic dermatitis, dysmenorrhea, and moderate anxiety reactions. There was significant clinical improvement in
all of the patients we treated.

Because of the somewhat surprising success with our use
of ultrasound in place of needles to apply acupuncture
therapy, we felt it imperative to report our preliminary findings. Ultrasound is a treatment modality of many years' dur-
ation and is familiar to general practice. Furthermore, we
feel ultrasound is an inherently safer procedure, especially in
the hands of practitioners unfamiliar with the use of the acupuncture needles.

This is a preliminary report on clinical findings and is not
meant to be a controlled study. In view of our findings, we

feel that controlled clinical trials of sonopuncture are indi-
cated.

So, what we are doing here is teaching people to let go of
time/space reality and to create an environment conducive to
making that possible. This requires a change, a reversal, in
what Western man has been taught. Instead of repressing the
natural hallucinations, fantasies and dreams, which arise
when we "space out" or alter our consciousness, we invite
these processes to manifest so that we may make friends with
them, and learn from them.

In the old days, back in the caves, we chose the one who
could see the best hallucinations and made that person holy.
In this manner a single brain, through its holographic discharges, controlled and guided the destiny of a whole tribe.
If I understand the hallucinogenic origins of the world's major religions correctly, the evolving brain structure continues
to direct and shape the destiny of all mankind. Where, for
example, did the Maharishi get the idea that a new golden
age of man is dawning?

Does it shape your own personal destiny? Does your own
three-million-year-old inherited brain structure alter your
very perceptions of reality in order to serve its own purposes?
In order to answer this question for yourself experientially,
look into holograms, particularly a laser light show, if possible. If you lean back and stop thinking (the auditory input
makes this easy) your brain will treat you to an incredible
series of three-dimensional color images, called holograms.
These images will be as real as any you have ever seen . . .
awake or asleep. They will be located somewhere behind
your eyeballs, in the space you usually call your "mind."
Your brain will create a three-dimensional image in response
to slightly differing sense impressions from each eye. This
phenomenon is called "binocular vision." It is a trick your
brain plays on you to make you think you are living in a
three-dimensional world. Actually it is just as likely that you

are projecting a three-dimensional reality as it is that you are
sensing or receiving one. Try it yourself. Seeing is believing.

Cover one eye, and look at your visual world. It's flat. It
has only two dimensions and no depth at all. This is true no
matter which eye you cover. Open both eyes, and you have
the illusion of depth. Reality flashes a two-dimensional picture at each eye. Creation of three-dimensional space out of
these two flat images occurs entirely within the brain and is
projected into the mind.

John Ross of University of Australia, writing in *Scientic
American*, March 1976, offers the theory that "The visual
system in effect constructs three-dimensional scenes from the
two-dimensional images formed on the retinas by fitting the
visual information into a conceptual framework." What we
see is a series of separate events, occurring in linear time
within a three-dimensional space. An interesting inference to
be drawn from this hypothesis is that the image of reality
flashed to you by your brain ain't necessarily so. To prove
his theory, Professor Ross devised an interesting experiment.
Using computers, oscilliscopes, a random number generator,
mirrors and a pair of lenses, he flashed a series of paired,
flashing dots into each eye of an observer. Much like looking
at a pair of "snowing" TV sets . . . one with each eye. "The
points of light appear briefly on the oscilliscopes. For each
point on the left screen, there is a corresponding point on the
right screen. The observer sees thousands of points of light
appearing and disappearing at random . . .

*The observer perceives the displays as a single scene in
vivid depth, with objects standing free in space.*

Looking into the machine everyone saw a three-dimensional square.

Not only did the observer's brain construct for him a 3D
square where there were only light flashes, it constructed a
perfect ideal square. There were points of light racing about
in an aimless swarm inside the square as well as outside the
square. The two did not mix since every time a point of light
in the swarm hit the border of the square it bounced off and
did not cross it. Which is really amazing since there was no

square and no border and no moving lights. Professor Ross believes;

"We must conclude that binocular perception has access to records of visual input that are independent of what we see."

These records of visual input are at least two. They are your belief as to what you *should* see. This belief has the ability to suppress what you actually *do* see, if it does not conform to the belief. The other influence on what you see and think is real is the memory of all the visual impressions harbored in your three-million-year-old brain.

Applied Alchemy—
A Rediscovered Healing Technique

The Food and Drug Administration announced that fifteen people had been killed by Clindamycin and Lincomycin "which are often prescribed by doctors for the treatment of acne and the common cold." The same federal agency warned that tolbutamide, a drug being taken daily by thousands of diabetics was capable of inducing fatal heart attacks. It was obvious to us that we needed a better approach to the problems of diabetes, acne, and the common cold. Bolstered by the admonition of Linus Pauling that, "progress in any science is based on a heretical view of both doctrine and authority," we decided to push ahead with our experiments at the clinic.

We were encouraged as well by a restaurateur named Tony.

"I'm seventy-nine years old. My wife, she just died from diabetes. What am I gonna do with myself? I committed suicide. I drank two water glasses full of whiskey, turned on the gas, tied a plastic bag over my head, and went to bed. In the morning, I woke up and looked out. It was quiet . . . nobody around. I thought I was dead so everyone else must be too. I took off the bag, opened the windows and turned off the gas so the place wouldn't blow up. For a whole hour I thought I was dead . . . until I saw people come into the street." Tony's trip to the edge of death had cured his depression and changed his life. "It's just like a caterpillar changing into another form. Since then I don't take no shit from no one—I figure I'm dead anyhow. God put me here to run a restaurant. Now I have to teach someone else what I learned. I buy whiskey by the case and keep running a restaurant because that is what I'm supposed to do."

Twenty-eight-year-old Robbie, who had been quietly sipping beer in Tony's restaurant, joined the conversation abruptly. "I'll believe this all-in-your-head stuff when I can make that ant up on the ceiling fall down." For about ten minutes, he sat quietly; deeply engrossed in his glass of beer. He was disturbed by a clinking sound in the bowl directly in front of him. In the bowl, crawling over the fruit, was the ant! We had both seen it fall and agreed that the odds against mechanical coincidence causing that particular ant to fall at that specific moment in time were astronomical. Robbie opened his eyes as wide as he could, did a Chaplin type of double-take as he stared at the ant. Smiling broadly, he stood up and raised his arms over his head, waggling his hands back and forth. He turned and strode away from the table saying, "I believe, I believe," still waggling his palms.

The possibility that Robbie made that ant fall cannot be discounted. If we admit that possibility we may safely say that we had witnessed an example of psychokinesis . . . (the ancients called it magic).

"I've seen people do something like that on the TV," says Tony. "This minister gets people all worked up; then he slaps them on the forehead and yells real loud: 'In the name of Jesus Christ, BE HEALED!'

"One old woman had arthritis so bad . . . couldn't move her arm for five years . . . my wife had it in her hip so I know . . . . When he grabbed her by the forehead and yelled 'BE HEALED!' she raised that crippled arm right up in the air and waggled it just like Robbie there . . . only she was yelling 'I'm healed! I'm healed!' He did it like an assembly line, one after the other; all waggling and yelling and claiming to be healed."

Joining in the camaraderie, I offered, "I read an article in *Medical Economics* about a religious lady named Olga Worral who can grab a breast tumor and make it disappear before your very eyes. She gets referrals from doctors all over the country. She claims to heal ninety percent of everyone who comes to her. She doesn't yell; she says she just lets the healing power of God flow through her body.''

Frank the fireman from the city wants to know if I really believe that shit. I tell him that I can only consider that shit as data to be evaluated according to the scientific method.

Robbie reads us a passage from his book. It is *Island* by Aldous Huxley. The scientific method is a way of looking at things, he says; ''. . . pure contemplation, unconcerned, beyond contingency, outside the realm of moral judgments. The scientific method requires dispassionate examination of the data.''

I remind them, "The data suggests that people are being healed by psychokinesis. We have to come up with a theory which explains that data. We can't close our eyes and yell fake. Healings like that have appeared in medical and lay literature since the time of Hermes." Frank the fireman from the city wants to know if I have a theory. I tell him that I don't, but the alchemists did.

"What was it?" he asks.

"They think it's somehow related to underwater sex."

The picture of the King and Queen copulating suggests an exchange of energy between the mind and body. The alchemical stone (wholeness or healing) is said to be found in its opposite; the state of chaos in which mind and body are in conflict. This is the state we call disease. The cure is to be found in the symptom. If we assume that cure and symptom are a pair of opposites, they must be part of a unity. If they are two versions of the same event, the one can be turned into the other. Intercourse occurs between the male mind and the female body as a form of energy flow which can travel in either direction. (The description here refers only to the mind and body of the patient under treatment.) Starting with the symptom as the *prima materia* the alchemical nuptials proceed.

When the mind and the body have been immersed in the world of pure energy, the patient is advised to ask the body to send a mental image which pictures the chief complaint. A case history will illustrate the procedure.

Lela has a bad right knee. It keeps her from doing things by unexpectedly slipping out from under her. She also gets pain when she walks or stands a great deal. It hurts more when she tries to straighten it out. She consulted an orthopedist who thinks that she might have a torn cartilage. "He wants me to go into the hospital so he can stick a needle into it and inject some dye." This procedure, she was told, would confirm the provisional diagnosis of a torn semilunar cartilage. "When I recover from that, he'll put me back into the hospital and cut my knee open and remove the cartilage." The patient and her mother have both studied Silva Mind Control. They are very good at making pictures in their heads.

I tell her, "Picture your problem as you would describe it to a four-year-old child." This is necessary because the form-making right cerebral hemisphere which contains the body image has very limited verbal ability.

"The bones in my knee are loose. When I walk, they slam against each other and hurt . . . sometimes they slip apart and I fall down." The patient is told to relax and, as with other patients, asked to enter the energy world and to see the floppy knee in her mind's eye.

In the waiting room, Lela's mother turns off time/space (using the method she learned at the mind control course) and pictures the same knee. "Make an equally simple picture of how it would look if it was fixed." The mother imagines little men installing foam rubber pads between the bones, and fixing them securely so they can't slip.

Lela, on the treatment table, imagines herself in a room and watches for a figure to appear. "It looks like a woman is coming in the door. She seems to be dressed in blue. She says her name is Kim."

"Assume she is real, treat her with respect, and ask her if she knows about your problem with the knee."

"She says she did that to attract my attention. She is trying to tell me something."

"Ask her what she is trying to tell you, and ask her advice as to how to heal the knee."

Kim thinks that Lela should not always do things just because people ask her to. "Every time you do that, I bang you in the knee." Kim further advises Lela to cancel the dye injection; she recommends a week of hanging around the house and staying off the leg.

"Ask her if she thinks you two should meet regularly."

"She thinks it would be a good idea if I would meditate fifteen minutes a day so we could chat about any problems which come up." Lela was also aware of the presence of a male image, "but he seems mild mannered, and agrees with Kim."

A week later, the patient stated that her symptoms were "seventy-five percent improved. I called the orthopedist and told him I wanted to understand the meaning of my symptom. Suppressing it only makes it come back worse in another form." The orthopedist was glad she felt better, but he was sure that psychiatry could never heal a torn cartilage. To the matter oriented mind, psychiatry is some sort of mumbo jumbo which is reserved for treatment of crazies and assorted neurotics who aren't really sick.

"I hung around the house and meditated three times a day like we agreed." All pain on standing has disappeared. "There is only a slight soreness in my knee when I stand for a long time." There was a one day relapse when she went to the airport at the insistence of a friend. "Kim thinks I should go to our house in the country. I'll have to watch my kid brother, but she says that's O.K."

Lela said goodbye and thanked us for our help. A month later we received the following note:

Dear Dr. Oyle,
    Regarding Lela whom you treated last month; she seems quite recovered.
    Thank you very much. (Had a great game of tennis with her yesterday.)

                                        Sincerely,
                                        Doris (Mother)

Psychiatry couldn't heal a ruptured semilunar cartilage;

apparently alchemy could! As a general practitioner, I am supposed to help humans heal quickly and with a minimum of fuss. As long as a procedure gets results, I don't care if you call it psychiatry, sonopuncture, or magic. I have chosen the name "applied alchemy"; but that says absolutely nothing about the event as seen by the mind.

That evening on television I saw pictures of a one thousand dollar missile destroying a two million dollar tank, and heard a physicist named Feynman say that whenever our view of things gets complicated, we should assume we are wrong. (I thought of the story of the fifteen deaths from acne treatment.) Dr. Feynman was saying that the observed behavior of subatomic particles moving at high speeds presented a serious challenge to current theories of how the world got to be like it is. "It seemed like new ideas were needed, so I started to think of new ideas." One of his new ideas was the Feynman Diagram which suggests that particles can move backwards in time. "Nature is exquisitely simple. The mind of the scientist tends to complicate it." Albert Einstein expressed the same emphasis on simplicity when he said: "The simpler our picture of the external world, and the more facts it embraces, the stronger it reflects in our mind the harmony of the universe."

THE PANACEA

"What's becoming clear is that we are all, doctors and patients, plugged into a set of concepts which, clutched to the end, limit and hurt us—the body as machine, to be acted on by drugs or knives; body and mind as separate; sickness as a malfunctioning in the machine, to be eliminated; doctors and patients in an unequal, manipulative relationship." My colleague, Leon, "dropped out" after eleven years as a general practitioner. These years were marked by what he called "a nagging sense of futility. An endless weight of pain I could only numb, suffering I could only turn away from . . . I only knew that I wanted out . . . It's of no use to make ultimate distinctions between psychic and physical disease, or between the various 'disease entities' within these categories. Diseases are not 'entities' at all; not solid realities dumped on us by whatever agent serves as the *cause* in our current theories . . . 'Disease entities' are merely different styles of fragmentation—different modes of suffering.'' Leon thinks we should make the basic assumption that ''health is our nature—if we allow it.'' He feels that applied alchemy is a promising modality for the general practitioner, and he would like to participate in the research.

Shortly thereafter, we come across the case of Susan, age twenty-four. She had hurt her back in a tumbling accident some ten years ago. Since then she has had recurrent attacks of severe, disabling back pain. The episodes of pain last about one month, and recur about every four months. Her last hospitalization was at age nineteen, when she spent three weeks in pelvic traction. Her back still hurts and she doesn't want to go through the agony of another hospitalization.

''O.K. Here we have an evolving mind/body. The mode of suffering chosen in this case is crippling intermittent back pain. The suffering is a message concerning the evolution of the mind/body in time and space. According to the paradigm postulated by the alchemists, the message is the cure as well as the suffering.''

Susan has been studying self-hypnosis and is very good at making pictures in her head. She can convert the symptom into an image. We'll try to convert the image into a cure.

Wholeness or healing is said to consist of four elements . . . *any* four elements as long as they represent two pairs of opposites. We could name the four elements of wholeness (health or unity), fire, water, air, and earth as in the realm of nature; or we could describe two pairs of opposing *qualities*: hot vs. cold and moist vs. dry, for example. A pair of warring opposites are to be placed in a hermetically sealed vessel, immersed in water and subjected to its opposite: fire. They will copulate; and healing will be the result of that mating.

Susan's warring body and mind are placed into a closed treatment room. She is left alone for ten minutes and advised to immerse them in a light hypnotic trance by imagining oceanic energy waves traveling over her body. In order to promote intercourse between the body and the mind, we then apply fire in the form of high frequency sound.

"When I ask my body to make a picture of my pain I see two tightly clenched fists pressing against each other·" She imagines herself in her own special place and looks around. "I see an old man in an old brown suit with a cane and a vest. He's sitting on a chair, looking at me . . . he just sits there and watches me."

"Ask him about your back."

"He says I should breathe and warm up the squeezed fists." She breathes regularly and slowly as advised by the little old man whose name is "Poppa." He tells her to concentrate all her attention on the pain. "Don't fight being— let the fists liquefy." When she asks for help, he hands her a candle and tells her to heat the fists until they liquefy. She is then left alone for ten minutes to continue heating and liquefying the fists. After the treatment, she said that she had a hard time saying goodbye to little old imaginary Poppa. "When I told him I felt bad because my left leg is a half inch shorter than my right leg, he said he also has a short leg— that's why he uses a cane. He said it doesn't bother him so why should it bother me. She left saying her back felt "really good," and she planned to meet with the old man in meditation for fifteen minutes three times a day.

Up to this point, Susan has converted the symptom into an image. The image seems to have effected healing. The requirement that she evolve in time and space has not yet been met. We may expect the symptoms to recur.

As expected, she returns about eight weeks later in severe pain, with decreased reflexes in her leg, and beginning atrophy of the calf muscle. She has been in the hospital for the past month with a diagnosis of a slipped or ruptured spinal disc. Two surgeons agree that her only hope for relief lies in a spinal operation.

As with Lela, "They want me to go into the hospital so they can stick a needle into my back and inject some dye."

She is describing myelography, which is a dangerous, painful and expensive diagnostic procedure. "When I recover from that, they'll put me back into the hospital and cut my spine open so they can remove the disc." The attack hit her in Texas at her grandmother's funeral. When she told the surgeon that she would like to try to cure her back through meditation, he told her that if she kept fooling around with unorthodox medical procedures, her leg would continue to shrivel up, and she would be crippled for life. When she insisted, refusing the myelogram, he became enraged. "You'll be back, you'll see, you'll be back on your knees, begging me to operate. Then I might not be willing to do it . . . just to teach you a lesson."

The totality of treatment (like every other totality) is composed of four parts. Ten minutes alone in the treatment room getting into the energy world, ten minutes of sonopuncture, ten or more minutes of talking to the images suggested by the symptom. The final period is spent in the waiting room discussing the results with the physician and anyone else who happens to be around.

Poppa reappeared to Susan complaining that she had not talked to him for almost eight weeks—since the death of her grandmother. Asked how Susan could be free of suffering, he said: "Be simple!"

"Ask him what you can do right now to relieve the pain."

Susan reports Poppa's response, "Flow energy, your liver is frozen. You froze it so as not to feel pain. Now you have to flow energy through it to thaw it. Breathe through the center of your body." Based on Poppa's diagnosis of a frozen liver, we administer high frequency vibratory fire into the liver source point on Susan's left foot.

"He's taking his overcoat off. He says he's warming up. He wants me to feel the energy from the sound machine and make it move round my body in a circle. My back feels like warm sun on melting snow . . . he thinks I should call him Grandpoppa."

"Ask him what he was trying to tell you in Texas when your back went out." Once again Susan relays his response.

"It was silly . . . you went there trying to find your childhood. It's not in Texas, it's in you. You have to throw a garbage can full of junk out of your head. After grandma died, you spent fifteen minutes three times a day reciting the prayer for the dead. I was right there beside you, and you never even noticed me." When she was ready to leave, Susan was given a written prescription which read as follows:

Rx: Meditation.

Directions: Take three times daily for one week.

She felt well after this for a period of four to five days. A week later she returned. A pain had developed in her right foot over the past two days, and was still present. She pointed to a spot on her leg which Grandpoppa had suggested we treat. We treated that point, and she left feeling greatly improved. She had avoided a surgical procedure and seemed well on her way to recovery.

A month later she was back as bad as ever. There was a shooting pain which radiated down her left leg as far as the ankle. She was unable to get pain free in any position and complained of numbness on the outside of the left thigh.

We agreed to treat her again only if she would agree to see our orthopedic consultant, a crackerjack surgeon who had decided he would no longer operate on people. During the course of treatment, Grandpoppa was joined by a pretty young woman named Liza. Susan saw a picture of her numb and painful leg as congested on the outside, but hollow and black on the inside. For immediate pain relief Liza suggested that Susan picture the leg filling with the sound energy and turning white on the inside. Asked to interpret the message in this relapse, Liza said, "You are too serious. Spring is a time to flounce." Ten days later, the leg felt better, but she had "an energy block the size of a football" in her left sacroiliac joint. Liza said this was to let her know she was not in balance with herself.

This time she advised melting the obstruction by circulating warm water around it. "Imagine the block is a lump of chocolate which melts as the warm water flows around it. Circulate the water up the front, down your back (through the chocolate), out your feet, into the sea, and out with the tide." During this procedure Susan commented, "I really feel alive!"

A week later we had a consultation report from our conservative orthopedic surgeon. He felt that there was no alternative to surgical intervention in this case since there was evidence of slowly progressive nerve damage. During the treatment Liza insists she wants to "keep bopping around" and Grandpoppa huddles silently in the corner saying nothing. Terrified by the prospect of spinal surgery, Susan and Liza agree to three weeks of absolute bed rest. It will be sort of a retreat from her life in time and space. Grandpoppa beams his approval. After a week of complete rest in bed the patient returns for a checkup and another treatment. She tells me, "We had a conference last week, and decided that this time we would fix the back properly. I agreed to consult with them regularly . . . especially when I'm under any sort of strain or tension."

During the treatment, Susan imagines two doctors entering her spine and pushing the herniated disc off the spinal nerve and back between the vertebrae where it belongs. This procedure results in immediate relief of pain. Liza then climbs down the spinal column and cements the disc into place. Susan spends nine more days in bed, and comes back feeling no pain. The numbness is gone and we can find no signs of disc trouble on physical examination. Susan feels she is cured. Her personality has changed. She says she is not as serious as she was, and flounces a good deal more.

"We're a family now. Every night before I go to sleep we chat about the problems of the day and they offer me guidance . . . I guess that's what Christ meant when He said "the kingdom is within." About six weeks later she returns for a checkup and a tuneup. She is completely symptom free and is sure she will never have trouble with her back again.

I wonder what would have happened if I had suddenly grabbed her by the forehead and yelled. "In the name of Hippocrates, BE HEALED!" . . .

PART TWO: FOR ISIS
Your Right Cerebral Hemisphere

"Rational consciousness . . . is but one special type of consciousness, whilst all about it, parted from it by the flimsiest of screens, there lie potential forms of consciousness entirely different. We may go through life without suspecting their existence; but apply the requisite stimulus, and at a touch they are there in all their completeness."

William James, A.D. 1902

The Decline and Fall of the Headlands Healing Clinic

Zelda qualifies for membership in three groups calling themselves "oppressed minorities." As a "female chicano psychic," she is in the same boat as Sammy Davis Jr., who calls himself "a one-eyed black jew." The local social worker, emissary of the Cartesian authorities, decided one day that (because of her membership in the last two categories) she was an "unfit mother."

He came into the clinic and told Zelda he was going to make her children wards of the court and place them in a foster home. Her reaction was entirely appropriate to the situation, screams of fury could be heard outside the clinic building.

The worker is the thirty-year-old divorced son of a conservative policeman. He wore a beard for a while but shaved it off just before confiscating Zelda's two daughters. A socially prominent local lady with two children of her own took the girls in.

Acting "to protect the children," *the county* split the family, and cut off financial aid to the mother.

"When you find a place to live, you can have the girls back," says *The Worker* (social).

"How can I find a place to live if you cut off my income?" asks *The Client*.

"Our prime responsibility is the protection of the children," says *The Supervisor* (of *The Worker*).

"It's the law," says *The Administrator*.

"How do you like my extended family?" asks *The Foster Parent*.

The Children, ages ten and twelve, are not asked for an opinion.

. . . . Zelda cries a lot . . . .

The TV carries stories of people running naked through the streets. A judge finds that "Streaking does not constitute indecent exposure unless the offender points to or otherwise indicates the genitals."

Zelda will get a *legal aid society* lawyer, and fight the action of *The State*.

Thirtyish and divorced, her life is balanced between the primal drives of devoted motherhood and the sensual urges of archetypal woman. "They all hate me in this gringo town because I have too much fire. My body is beautiful and I don't have to hide it—I'm a triple Leo, you know; that's a lot of fire. My emotions are too strong for them . . . I have a lot of trouble because of my emotions . . . When they get me too mad or upset, I have to drink to calm myself, sometimes I drink so much I don't know what I'm doing and I fall down. Then they take me to the hospital and fill me full of Thorazine. When they give me that stuff, I have no emotions, no feelings, no nothing."

Guided by intuition and her visions, she has raised two well-adjusted, happy, outgoing daughters. They are both doing well at school and have learned to shepherd their mother through most of her emotional crises. These episodes usually manifest in the course of her dealings with WASP men. ("They get mad because I pay too much attention to the girls.") For the past year, she has been able to stay out of the hospital and to deal more effectively with the volcano of her affectivity (emotionality). She comes into the clinic for a sonopuncture treatment whenever she feels an impending explosion, about two or three times a month. The treatment consists of the administration of a beam of high frequency sound into her acupuncture meridian system, via the appropriate points. The Chinese feel that the five basic emotions: fear, anguish, joy, anger and obsession are faces of a single life energy which they call " chi." The flow of chi balances and regulates the emotions, they suggest.

Following the fifteen-minute treatment, she is left alone to disperse the accumulated excess. This is usually accomplished by pounding on the treatment table, swearing, and/or wailing loudly. After ten minutes she comes out; smiling and composed . . . able to continue her normal activities.

Zelda's confrontation with the System and the Social Worker was precipitated by an altercation with her landlord. "He said that if I didn't do what he wanted me to, he would throw me out of the house and see to it that the girls were taken away from me. That faggot bastard thinks that he can do anything he wants just because he is rich and important. He called the welfare department and told them that I tried to kill him and was threatening to kill the children and myself."

She had come in for a treatment, and met the social worker in the waiting room. Her reaction to his announced intentions left him pale, shaken, and convinced that she was a menace to society in general and to her children in particular. "I always knew she was crazy . . . besides, if I don't act on the complaint and she harms the girls, I could lose my job." Sam is a triple Scorpio, recently divorced, and into "approaching women in an open, direct manner." It is Zelda's opinion that "if he can't screw me at home, then he'll get his rocks off by fucking me over in court."

The judge decides that since Zelda has not harmed her daughters over the past twelve years, she is unlikely to do so at the present time . . . Change, it seems, is in the air.

The daughter of an embarrassingly wealthy Scarsdale-type matron appears on a three-hour NBC prime time special called "The Changing Relationship Between Men and Women." "I really love to have sex," she tells an audience of thirty million viewers. Her quest for sexual fulfillment has been dedicated and uncompromising. "When I meet a new man, I feel I must experience him fully . . . I have tried every conceivable type of sexual activity," . . . even orogenital relations, which she does not find at all distasteful. In an audience of thirty million Americans, someone is sure to have found it necessary to wrestle with the question, "Mommy, what does 'orogenital relations' mean?" The female interviewer, her face immobilized in an expression of icy objectivity, gives our little interviewee a question of her own to wrestle with. "What, in your opinion is the difference between you and what used to be called a tramp?"

Like beauty, morality seems to be in the eye and the mind of the beholder. Maybe *everything* is in the beholder's mind and/or eye? Consider what happens to empirical reality after three ounces of booze, 400 micrograms of lysergic acid diethylamide, or after a joint of good Colombian weed containing a significant amount of tetrahydracannabinol. The world seems different, doesn't it? Oh no, you may say, it only *looks* different. The world out there is real enough; a chemical changes one's view of that real world so it looks different. The drug merely alters the way in which the sense organs report what we call reality . . . my car, my body, etc. Well, it ain't necessarily so! Let us consider the visual world. Our eyes, we are told, like binocular cameras, receive light waves bouncing off some real object out there. A lens and shutter arrangement, they regulate the intensity of the reflected light waves and focus them on the retina to form an image. The retina acts like the film in the camera. The optic nerve, like a TV cable, carries that image to the visual cortex and up to the higher centers of consciousness where we theoretically reproduce an image of the thing out there . . . only the image is completely "in here"; inside the skull. This inside image is ultimately all your consciousness can deal with. Whatever it is that is really out there reflects the state of your eyes, your retina, your nervous system, and finally the state of your perceiving consciousness. The reality of the thing reflecting the light is unknowable in the objective sense. It may be that only the image is real . . . perhaps the whole thing is happening on the back of your eyeballs.

Zelda showed her gratitude by becoming the "cleaning lady" for the clinic building. That was the beginning of the end for the Headlands Healing Service. The clerk of the Session of the church, an incredibly clean little, old man with an impeccably white BMW automobile sent us a letter: "The Session of the Calvary Presbyterian Church feels the need for a new minister," he lied, adding that we were to vacate the premises within thirty days. "We trust that this will not inconvenience you," he lied again. He understood the concern of the staff who asked for time to relocate in order to fulfill our obligations to patients still in treatment, but he felt that property rights must take precedence over mere considerations like medical abandonment.

It is December, almost the shortest day of the year. As has been our custom we seek the advice of the *I Ching*. We draw the hexagram called "Darkening of the Light." The advice contained therein is, as usual, sound and precisely relevant to the situation. The trigram representing Earth is above, and the trigram for fire is below. The oracle speaks clearly and explicitly.

"Here the sun has sunk under the Earth and is therefore darkened . . . a man of dark nature is in a position of authority and brings harm to the wise and able man . . . In a time of darkness it is essential to be cautious and reserved. One should not needlessly awaken overwhelming enmity by inconsiderate behavior . . . In social intercourse one should not try to be all knowing. One should let many things pass without being duped."

The changing line, which gives additional advice, is even more explicit: "We find ourselves close to the commander of darkness and so discover his most secret thoughts. In this way we realize that there is no longer any hope of improvement, and thus we are enabled to leave the scene of the disaster before the storm breaks."

Off the walls come medical degrees, practice licenses, internship certificates, anatomical charts, and all the things which make a storage room look like a treatment room. Books, treatment tables, the sterilizer, disposable syringes and scalpels are claimed by their new owners. The telephone is disconnected (no forwarding number). The door is locked and the key is thrown into the Pacific Ocean. A newspaper on the floor gravely announces that six and a half million Americans are unemployed, and the rate is expected to go significantly higher. The henchmen of the deposed and disgraced ex-president have been found guilty of a conspiracy to establish a dictatorship in the United States.

The dance of Shiva, like Shakespeare's tempest in a teapot, full of sound and fury, signifying nothing, increases its tempo.

Mr. Craggs, of the firm of Snodgrass and Craggs, is a pillar of the community. S. & C. is a highly respected establishment-type law firm deeply rooted in the traditions of the nineteenth and early twentieth century. His client, the Session of the Calvary Presbyterian Church, is a matriarchy deeply rooted in the traditions of the Middle Ages. Three days into the last quarter of the twentieth century Mr. C. (of S. & C.) informs the Headlands staff that the church ladies are of the opinion that a loose woman (Zelda) has been living in the clinic building with her two daughters and practicing prostitution out of the staff office. The Headlands Healing Service is closed and bankrupt; Zelda is living in a town five miles away, but the crusade continues.

Mr. Muzzy, on the advice of his counsel, has written a letter to the License Department on the stationary of the Presbyterian Synod of the Pacific. As Finance Director, he has requested that the license of the now defunct clinic be revoked. "After all," he apologized, "when you consult a lawyer, you do what he tells you to do." In 1971 when the Synod Officials agreed to sponsor the Headlands Project a group of ministers in the Church World Interaction Committee thought it might make the local Presbyterian Church more relevant to the life of the community.

"There's been a change of administrations." He explains that the previous administration aroused the ire of the local church folk by donating $10,000 to the Angela Davis Defense Fund. Angela Davis, a black female communist, was not well regarded by the local church folk. The new officials while not officially rescinding the original agreement are not sure what is going on.

The local Presbyterian Church Ladies, for their part, are out for blood and the witch hunt begins.

Bolinas, a far-out little town of about 1500 people is not on the map. To further insure its inaccessibility the local residents have removed all the road signs from the main highways. It has been identified by county officials as a mental institution run by the inmates. *The Hearsay News* is a mimeographed-in-blue-ink local weekly tabloid which carried the following items on page 3.

12/4/74

Open Letter to the Editor,
Dear Sir,

I would like to clarify what seems to be a misunderstanding by some members of the Bolinas community about the current conflict between the Headlands Health Clinic and Calvary Presbyterian Church.

When the clinic was seeking space some time back, the church agreed to let its manse be used. There was no hidden agenda, no secret agreement. It was an open rental agreement free to be terminated by either party on written notice.

Now the church wishes to use the manse for its own program. It submitted written notice to Dr. Oyle of that fact. Dr. Oyle's attitude has been: I'm here. I can't relocate. Get me out if you can. Consequently the church has had to seek legal counsel.

I find it difficult to understand why Dr. Oyle is acting as if he were an injured party with no obligation to honor the wishes of the church to regain the use of its own property.

> *Sincerely,*
> *A local citizen*

*Open Letter **FROM** the Editor:*
Dear local citizen,

> *I would like to clarify what seems to be a mis-understanding by you about editors:*
> *They are not all "sirs."*
> > *Sincerely,*
> > *Mary Lowry*
> > *Friday Editor, Hearsay News*

Another local citizen with a "Jesus Saves" sign on his trunk arrives and announces triumphantly that the license of the clinic has been revoked. A large man in flowing robes with a huge crucifix dangling from a rope around his neck gets off a bus the next Sunday morning and performs an exorcism on the empty building.

We approached the firm of Ginsburg, Ginzburg and Ginsburg to defend the nonexistent Headlands Healing Service. The firm had been busily engaged recently defending a young man accused of stealing some very important papers from one Daniel Ellsberg, another prominent personality.

At our first meeting in the firm's offices, wiry, white haired Mr. G., senior partner of G. G. & G. was pissed because the sheriff brought his client, the defendant in that case, into court in bare feet. The judge, in a wheelchair, (with wounds incurred in a gun battle during which he shot and killed three of his fellow humans) agrees to take the matter under advisement.

Mr. G. looks like Clarence Darrow as he blows off steam. "Those bastards . . . just because he couldn't afford bail . . . they do that all the time . . . to make him look guilty . . . they know that judge freaks if someone comes into his court without a tie . . . barefoot! Can you imagine that! Those sons of bitches!''

Noticeably turning his mind to more pleasant matters he leafs quickly through the evening paper, and with a wry smile confides, ''My name's not in the obituary column again today! Now then, what can I do for you?''

The issue is joined in the local Judicial District Court in and for the County of Marin, January 3, Nineteen Hundred and Seventy-Five. This information is important, since it implies that the events described transpired within what we call time and space.

Representing the church ladies along with their attorney, the distinguished and supremely confident Mr. Craggs, were two witnesses, the incredibly clean little old man and Big Jerry, the probation officer, who pinch-hit as minister to the congregation.

Opposing this imposing array of nineteenth century protestant power was ''young Richard,'' a junior partner in the firm of G. G. & G. Young Richard's only witness was the author, who, at that time, was the ex-director of the extinct clinic. On the bench was Judge Sternly, looking down on everything as he absentmindedly cleaned the dirt from under his fingernails.

The unbelievably clean little old man testified that the building was occupied by ''unauthorized persons,'' and the tenants neglected to cut the grass behind the building and allowed weeds to accumulate around the butane tank behind the church. He also complained of the accumulation of great numbers of whiskey bottles outside the back door.

Big Jerry, the probation officer, when asked if he preferred to be called ''Reverend'' smiled benignly and said, ''Jerry is O.K.'' He testified that as minister to the congregation of the Calvary Presbyterian Church he had the use of the three-bedroom manse which housed the Headlands Clinic and used to frequent the place occasionally on weekends. ''It just wasn't a good arrangement,'' he recalled. ''We would come out for a weekend of privacy and relaxation only to find that someone in the house during the week was using our stuff.''

Young Richard's defense was simple, direct and inept. Judge Sternly, his nails clean by now, noted that the defense counsel had long hair tied back in a Kung Fu type pigtail, and that the only witness for the defense had no tie. Glowering menacingly at us, he looked like an inquisitor defending mother church against her satanic enemies.

"When you occupy someone's building, you gotta pay rent or get out." He further pointed out that the whole clinic operation was illegal because no one from the synod had signed the application for a license. Apparently, in his considered opinion the patients whose treatment and well-being were threatened by the sudden closing of the clinic deserved no special consideration superseding the property rights of the plaintiff. He would take the entire matter under advisement, as was his custom, and render a verdict at a later date. At this writing, the verdict has not yet been forthcoming.

That same evening, the NBC Nightly News reported on the reaction of one Kenneth Parkinson to his acquittal after a long and grueling trial. Indicted, along with four older members of the Nixon cabal, clean-cut Kenneth established his innocence and narrowly avoided a jail sentence. At stake were a promising career and an ego nurtured on the ambrosia of seemingly limitless power. Existence in the role of a convicted felon, at the opposite pole of the power spectrum, would represent for young Ken, a psychic catastrophe equivalent to the loss of a limb.

Asked to comment on his experience, he replied, "Sitting in the car, after the trial, on my way home, with my wife next to me, I felt like I had just left a heavy movie."

Images, Events and Imaginings

I heard a bell, located the source, picked up the telephone and said "Hello" into the green plastic mouthpiece. "This is Sonoma State College" came out the other round plastic end. The little voice in my ear would like me to talk about the work we have been doing at the Headlands Clinic; it would like me to talk to a group of graduate nurses. "I would like you to present the topic 'Alternatives to Medicine' to my class later this month." The little voice identified itself as Mary Jane, Assistant Professor of Nursing. The Department of Nursing, it says, will provide reimbursement for my travel expenses and an Honorarium of $25. The little voice in my head is sure her students will be quite interested in my ideas and will be a responsive group. It also wishes to thank me personally for making this effort for the nursing department.

When the phone rang I had been reading the newspaper on the table in front of me which proclaimed an impending crisis in medicine. The doctors can't get malpractice insurance. "I won't even answer the telephone without malpractice insurance" (it says in the newspaper on the table in front of me). I guess that's why they're looking for alternatives to medicine, runs through my mind. "I'd rather talk about The New Medical Model," I say to the piece of green plastic in my hand. "Fine, see you then," it replies. I gently replace the receiver on its cradle.

The clinic has been closed for six weeks. Judge Sternly has rendered his decision ordering the corpse of the Headlands Clinic to pay thirteen hundred dollars because it took too long dying. The San Francisco Public Schools are also running out of money. It looks like unemployment and starva-

tion will run rampant for the next decade at least. Dick
Gregory is claiming he has proof that the CIA killed President Kennedy and my checks are beginning to bounce. I
don't want to go back into fee-for-service private practice. It
is early February and the days are getting longer. The light
power is on the rise. The old society is moribund, the promise of spring and the age of Aquarius stirs slightly. The *I
Ching* is open to hexagram #43, "Breakthrough."

It refers to, "a time when inferior people gradually begin
to disappear. Their influence is on the wane; as a result of
resolute action, a change in conditions occurs, a
breakthrough."

"That's all very fine," I think, "but what about the danger that the twentieth century will take us all down as it dies
. . . what about ten million starving humans in the world."

"The best way to combat evil is to make energetic progress
in the good," says the book. I guess Nero fiddled while
Rome burned because . . . what else was there to do under the
circumstances? Apparently Gerald Ford, playing golf as
Indo-China falls, agrees.

The green plastic telephone calls again. It is a female voice.
"I heard a tape of your talk at U. C. Santa Cruz. My gynecologist wants to do a hysterectomy. He says he saw some
premalignant cells on my cervix. Two Pap smears were negative, but he thinks my uterus should come out anyway for
safety's sake. I'm 45. My analyst is trying to help me do
some visual imagery techniques. I can't really get relaxed
enough to get into it. My husband (he's a furniture manufac-
turer) thinks I shouldn't fool around with all this occult mystical bullshit. I told him to listen to your tape, but he simply
refuses. I understand you have some kind of machine that
helps people relax. My husband says there's all kinds of
wierdos around with all kinds of stupid machines and he
thinks they're all quacks. The astrologer says it's because I
have some afflicted planets. My husband says it's the astrologer who's afflicted."

"The clinic is closed because we had trouble with the landlord," I tell the little green plastic machine. I explain to it
that the treatment technique we are developing at the clinic

must be considered to be in the experimental stages. I can't promise that it will cure the tumor, "Besides, I don't even have an office in which to treat patients."

The phone is silent for a moment before it continues, "I don't really see why I should be a guinea pig for an experiment and have to pay for it to boot. I don't have a tumor anyhow, only some premalignant cells. Maybe I should just go back to my etching and forget about the whole thing. My husband says I should do whatever I feel is best. My gynecologist says I have plenty of time to think about it. I can call him back in six weeks and have another checkup. I think I need a complete physical exam, but the internist says he can't see me until next month."

"I think you should do whatever you feel is best. I'm certain that you will make the right choice. Since you have no tumor at present and the gynecologist says there is no urgency, why don't you concentrate on your etching for a while and have him recheck you regularly. You only have to know that whatever you decide, you will be O.K."

"Thank you very much, I feel a great deal better. I'll send you an etching." It falls silent again, and I return to my newspaper.

A surgeon from Minnesota smiles benignly from the pages of the book review section. A magazine columnist, and a best selling author, he took it upon himself to conduct "a personal investigation of faith healers and psychic surgeons." At the outset, he began with "the genuine hope that he would find medical miracles—cures that could not be accomplished by orthodox practitioners of medicine." The reviewer accepts the doctor as "sincere whereas one might suspect the bias of other members of the profession." He has "established himself as something of a medical maverick, unbound by organized medicine's restrictions and customs." He is acutely aware of the limitations of his profession. He was unimpressed by the thin material the American Medical Association had accumulated to refute the claims of the miracle healers. He signed up as an usher at the services of the now late Kathryn Kuhlman, "a charismatic woman who appeared on the TV screen every Sunday to interview yet another person who has been healed of some dread disease or deformity at one of her miracle services." Sadly, he delivers his verdict. "I don't believe Miss Kuhlman is a liar; I don't believe she is a charlatan; I don't believe she is consciously dishonest. I think that she honestly believes the Holy Spirit works through her to perform miraculous cures. I think that she sincerely believes the thousands of patients who come to her services every year and claim cures are, through her ministrations, being cured of organic diseases."

He then makes the interesting if somewhat arrogant statement that although these "thousands of patients" claim to be cured, they really aren't . . . they only *think* they are cured. To be more exact, it is his contention that they only *thought* they were sick in the first place. "The problem," he says, "is one of ignorance." To prove this point he postulates a thoroughly disproven and discredited hypothesis. "Miss Kuhlman," he observes, "doesn't know the difference between psychogenic and organic diseases." The crushing weight of evidence which has been accumulating since the time of Einstein and Carl Jung suggests that the difference between "psychogenic" and "organic" disease does not exist outside the conventional wisdom of the surgeon's own materialistically oriented healing cult. Perhaps the good doctor is not as much of a "maverick" as he would have us believe.

"Miss Kuhlman doesn't know anything about hypnotism and the power of suggestion." He neglects to mention the fact that neither does he nor anyone else in the scientific community. The mode of action of these methods is only now being seriously explored throughout the world. Then he gives us a keen insight into the mental attitude of the members of *his* particular cult, projecting them onto Miss Kuhlman:

"It may be that she doesn't want to learn that her ministry is not as miraculous as it seems . . . she has trained herself to deny, emotionally and intellectually, anything that may threaten the validity of her ministry." Claiming that the cures achieved by "healers" are almost invariably in cases where the ailment is not what he calls "organic," he notes that "it is among those they cannot help that the 'miracle healers' (and *I* might add, surgeons) do their greatest injury." He then complains about "the delay, sometimes fatal, they cause by offering an easier cure for those afflicted who might be saved by surgery or other medical establishment procedures." Our fair-minded maverick has returned to the establishment corral, proclaiming the power of *his* cult to heal where others have failed!

Why then, we may ask, are patients by the thousands flocking to "faith healers" all over the world? His own profession, says the doctor, "sometimes fails to offer compassion and understanding and thus drives the desperate patient into the hands of the healers." He reluctantly concludes that "healers do not constitute a source of miraculous hope for the seriously ailing." (After twenty years of medical practice I must conclude just as reluctantly, "neither do surgeons.") He ends his book with a statement which indicates a hopeful increase in consciousness among establishment physicians (who consider themselves a cut above "healers").

"We don't need to seek out miracle workers if we're ill. To do so, is in a way, an insult to God. Our minds and bodies are miracle enough." I couldn't agree more.

Consider the case of Rebecca. She would like some help "getting her head together." She is pregnant and is interested in "getting in touch with myself so I can come to terms with this pregnancy." She runs a massage parlor in San Francisco; I can treat her there since I don't have an office. "I'd also like you to talk to my friend . . . she's a nurse; been having a lot of trouble with her back and she thinks the orthopedic surgeon has been screwing her around. If you come into the city, you can see us both on the same day." Rebecca is a strikingly beautiful twenty-five year old who greets me in a direct, no-nonsense manner. She sings with a rock and roll group and has just discovered that her uterus harbors a spark of life. "I can't possibly have a baby now, it will louse up my whole career. I want to have an abortion, but I feel terrible about destroying life."

"Can you make pictures in your head?"

"I sure can; 3D and in living color!"

She spends ten minutes relaxing on the massage table picturing herself in a clearing in the forest. "Just hang out there for a while and let me know if a creature appears." She says: "I see two lions, a male and a female." She observes that they are simply sitting there looking at her. As the sonopuncture starts she says, "They seem to like that, they're starting to frolic and play with each other."

"Will they talk to you about your conflict?" The lion nods his assent. "Ask them what they think about your dilemma."

"There's a butterfly, too. The male lion just grabbed it in his mouth. The female says she would never destroy one of her pups, but she has no compunction about destroying life in order to get food." The male tells her he can either swallow the butterfly or release it. It's all the same to him. He tells Rebecca that he thinks it is O.K. to destroy in order to create. "Destruction for its own sake is evil, destruction as a part of creation is not."

Destruction and creation are two sides of a single entity.

"What about the butterfly *you* swallowed? Are you going to destroy it or let it out?" That question makes her laugh heartily—even joyously. The lions tell her that they are there to help her. They will change forms from time to time, but anytime she has a problem she is to feel free to call on them and they will be there to help her with it. She will go into the hospital tomorrow for the abortion. "I've found something which will guide me through the rest of my life." As the man in the magazine article says . . . "Our minds and bodies are miracle enough."

Alexander Solzhenitsyn poses the problem. "How many human beings are there, now, at this minute, rushing about in mute panic, wishing they could find a doctor, the kind of person to whom they can pour out the fears they have deeply concealed or even found shameful? . . . the sort of thing you can't ask your friends for advice about. Nowadays it's easier to find a good wife (or husband) than a doctor willing to look after you personally for as long as you want, and who understands you fully and truly." Carl Gustav Jung proposes a solution: "Meditation . . . the name of an internal talk of one person with another who is invisible, as in the invocation of the Diety, or communion with one's self or with one's good angel." The two lions and Rebecca provide an example. The guru on the television commercial points to a can of 7-Up and says: "You seek the answer, my friend, LOOK INSIDE." The idea that we are to "look inside" and have an "internal talk" with an invisible person or creature suggests that we are dealing with events which take place entirely within your head. The thirteen and a quarter billion cells within have various techniques for communicating with (*insert your name*), the tip of the iceberg. For the visually oriented, they produce visions, dreams and hallucinations. For those who cannot "see," they emanate random thoughts, ideas, and inspirations. For the nonverbal they emit hunches and intuitions. For all of us they orchestrate the tides of emotion which color, direct, and often overpower our tiny arrogant spark of rationality. For the recalcitrant who believe only in rational thought and the materialistic "reality" of time and space they create pain, accidents, and disease. The purpose for all these devices is merely to attract your attention . . . and attract it they will, by any means necessary.

Suppose next time you feel an emotional charge or stub your toe, you don't name it or look for a reason. Suppose instead, you meditate on the events and look for a message. In the chapters which follow you are invited to experience a series of apparently disconnected juxtaposed events. Some seem to take place in the mind of the author, others are apparently set in time and space, while still others represent images appearing on the television screen in my home, or stories in the newspaper. If you simply experience these images with a relaxed, open mind you may become aware of a form which is different from and more than the sum of the separate incidents. The ability of your brain to fuse unrelated and incomplete data into a new insight is illustrated in the following diagrams. The experiment which follows may reproduce, on a cognitive level, the phenomenon which you will now experience on a visual level.

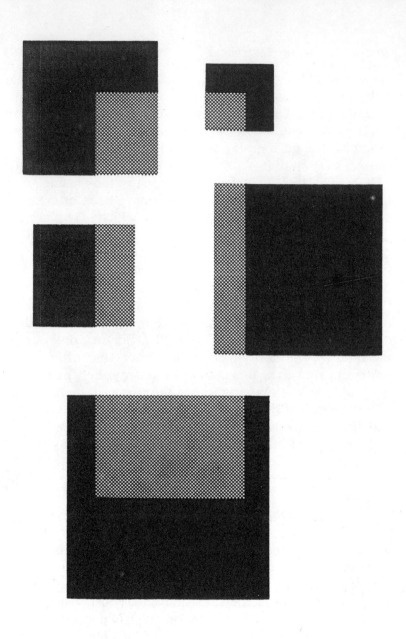

A gauze-like rectangle is superimposed on five black squares, or is it? The borders of the rectangle do not extend beyond the black squares.

The white on white borders do not exist. Examine them closely and they disappear. Your mind has imposed its own form on external reality. Note that the square persists even though you know it isn't there.

Four three-quarter circles and four two-sided angles equal one square hallucination. You are creating a form which connects eight separate events in the black space.

A rainy Sunday afternoon in mid February; it has been showering for ten days without letup. I join the teenagers, Julie, Fred and the twins, Abbie and Ben, watching ABC Wide World of Sports. A Russian weight lifter raises five hundred and thirty-five pounds off the floor and holds it over his head. The commentator notes that in the period immediately preceding the actual lifting, the athlete concentrates on the weight for a full three minutes. "It's as though he were making a mental picture of that weight rising. Many athletes have told me that they do that before attempting something difficult." He thinks that no human in history has ever lifted that much weight.

During the commercial break, there is an advertisement for a new porno movie which "has already been seen by one-sixth of the entire adult population of Paris."

"Do you know which is the most sensitive part of your body?" the commercial continues. "It's not the nape of your neck, your thigh, or your breast . . . It's *your mind*!"

Without warning, the TV picture switches. I am watching events which transpired in another time at a distant place; only here they are, in my living room! Here they are, before my eyes, right now! I am looking at the Seattle World's Fair of 1974. A group of masters from Taiwan, China, is going to give me a demonstration of "chi; the life force." For openers, a young oriental man about twenty-five years old blindfolds himself and jumps through a flaming circle of knives. "My God!" shouts the announcer, "no two of those knife tips were more than eighteen inches apart." Another young oriental man then comes out and places four bamboo sticks about four feet long and between one and two inches wide into circular strips of ordinary newspaper. The paper strips are suspended from the cutting edges of razor sharp swords held by four young Chinese maidens (two of whom were giggling uncontrollably). By means of kung fu, "a means of harmonizing mind, body, and the universe," the young man is able to break all four sticks with a fifth; without cutting or tearing the newspaper. "There's no trickery to this," says the announcer, "we checked everything beforehand."

In rapid succession, a man is smashed on the skull with a sledge hammer, another has the sharp edge of a sword driven against his bare chest with tremendous force, and yet another has a two by four broken over his bent back. There are no injuries. "The mind can generate chi, the life force which is the most powerful force we know. Chi, the life force does not come in neatly wrapped packages. It is the one universal force which we only know by experiencing its many faces."

"How do you suppose they do that, Howard?"

"Beats me!"

The scene shifts to Daytona Beach in Florida but our minds are not ready to part with what we have just seen. The concept of chi had been discussed a few nights earlier on TV by a well-known physicist who noted that scientists now feel that the four major forces known to man are all examples of a single universal force. Could that be the same as chi? The four forces known to man at present are gravity, electromagnetism (electricity and magnetic force), strong nuclear force and weak nuclear force (which has something to do with radioactivity and subatomic particles). The Russians call this single force bioplasmic energy. The ancient Egyptians called it serpent power. It is interesting to note that the totality of all forces known to man is always divided into four aspects. The physicist's four forces or elements are the fire, water, air and earth of the alchemists. The tendency to divide every known unity into four basic parts seems to be characteristic of the human mind.

My four teenagers have peripherally moved in and out of the conversation as they watch the cars zoom around the nonexistent race track on the TV screen. "They told me in high school that modern science has solved all the questions about the nature of our world. It looks to me like they haven't solved shit!"

Sixteen-year-old Fred agrees, "Yeah, remember all that business about Galileo? They were gonna torture him for saying that the earth revolves around the sun. He had to admit in public that he was wrong; it's really the sun that's moving, they made him say. My teacher said after he made the public announcement that the earth is stationary, he whispered under his breath that "it does move." My teacher tried to make out like Galileo was a scientist so I should believe him and not that bunch of backward religious fanatics. He never says how that jibes with Einstein's idea that absolute motion is impossible to determine. According to Einstein, they were both right and they were both wrong."

Fourteen-year-old Abbie is fascinated, "You mean, if I'm walking along, it's possible that I'm stationary, and the scenery is moving past me? That's pretty far out!"

The TV tuner clicks twice and flips us back through time and space to Stalin's Russia, to experience *The Lysenko Affair*. The paradigm clash depicted concerns the claims of a Soviet agrobiologist named Lysenko who maintained that the science of Mendelian genetics is "A capitalist plot to perpetuate the myth of racial superiority based on inheritance." Opposing him was a scientist named Popov who believed that only genes carry traits from one generation to the next. "Environmental changes are not inherited . . . only genetic mutations cause species or individual differences." The villain in this story was not the church, it was Godless Communism. Faced with ten million starving peasants after the revolution, the party ordered its scientists to produce a wheat which would survive the Russian winter by maturing before the weather became severe. Popov said it would take ten to twelve years of cross-breeding to produce the required strain. Lysenko claimed that "Plants will do whatever you want them to; you simply have to let them know what you want them to do." He produced a new cereal strain in two years. Popov claimed that it was a lucky accident . . . Lysenko was "only a farmer's son skilled in practical agriculture, and not, after all, a true scientist."

A pragmatist above all, Stalin elevated Lysenko to a high position, and clapped scientist Popov into a concentration camp where he subsequently died; another martyr to the cause of Holy Mother Science. "My teacher claims Lysenko was a quack. Acquired characteristics are never inherited."

"How does your teacher explain R factor plasmids?"

"He never heard of them. What are R factor plasmids?"

"When you give a patient broad spectrum antibiotics like ampicillin or tetracycline, the bugs develop a resistance to the drug. They pass this acquired resistance to their offspring through these things in the cell called R factor plasmids. It begins to look like they were both right."

"Don't tell that to my biology teacher. He's a goddam fanatic." In that case, he shouldn't pose as a scientist.

There is some discussion about the ability of the kung fu people to control the body with the mind. Lysenko maintained that he could direct the growth of wheat by using his mind. Suppose you could control the mind itself. If we agree for a moment that the mind tends to divide every totality into four parts, we may postulate that the mind shows four basic rhythms:

Beta	13 and up	thinking about things out there in time and space
Alpha	7 to 13	stoned in pure energy space with no thought
Theta	4 to 7	making pictures in your head
Delta	0 to 4	dead asleep (inside black nothing)

The comparable states in a TV receiver are: *Beta*—NBC Nightly News talking about a bomb which has just exploded in a TV studio; *Alpha*—making a hissing noise while the screen shows nothing; *Theta*—moving diagonal patterns with color pushed to maximum; and *Delta*—off. (A fifth state, the state of death is equivalent to a blown out color tube.)

"Nowadays, most people identify themselves almost exclusively with their consciousness. (They stay in beta almost constantly.) Our concepts of time and space have only approximate validity. We as a society put far too much emphasis on our experiences in the beta state and in the world of time and space. It's quite possible that it's only just another television show. (Time and space, that is.)

"If you see heavy tragedy, change the station and discover a light comedy." suggests Ben. "That's pretty far out."

"If all my experiences are television shows, who's producing them?" fourteen-year-old Abbie wonders.

"It may be some sort of resonance phenomenon. The mind when it's counting change in a supermarket is projecting beta waves; we can measure and record them. Do you know for sure that that same mind is not also projecting the supermarket, the change, and the counting fingers? Maybe the mind vibrates between projecting time/space and experiencing it."

Even Abbie agrees that dreams, memories and hallucinations are produced by the mind which perceives them. "But reality, things I can feel, and smell, and touch; I just can't believe that I'm making that up with my mind, too."

"You think something is 'real' if you can see it, feel it and smell it, right?"

"Right!"

"What about time, and space, are they real? Immanuel Kant thinks we make up time and space, and everything that they contain. In that case, everything you call real might be only a projection of your mind in 3D and in color . . . a hologram."

In that view, my life is simply a three-dimensional movie which I project with my mind. I simultaneously project it and receive it. Like a movie, it is a series of intermittent flashes or still pictures running at the rate of twenty-four frames per second giving the illusion of continuous action. Twenty-four frames per second, the rate at which most movie projectors run, is the rate at which the brain flashes during waking consciousness. (Beta rate—more than thirteen cycles or flashes per second.) "If I'm making it all up, why do I give myself so much hassle?"

The Buddhists, among others, think that "The cause for all human suffering lies in ignorance." We make up a crummy life experience because we don't realize that we're making it up. We look at the world around us make a picture or some thoughts about "the way it is," and that creates "the way it is." At this point, someone shuts off the TV, and I go to sleep. It all stops.

The next morning it's still raining, the moon is new, and it's Lincoln's birthday. A two-day-old newspaper is chatting about the state of our State's Health Care Delivery System. The article is entitled, SHE BEGGED AND WEPT FOR SON'S TREATMENT. The newspaper, leaning comfortably against a shoebox, says: Health Care Investigation May Reveal Expensive Scandal. It seems many people have traded valid medical insurance for membership in the Prepaid Health Plan (PHP), which has cost the state $343 million. Most of the money went for administrative expenses. "In one case, a doctor working as a "plan administrator" was paid $120,000 a year." The article, "She Begged and Wept for Son's Treatment," describes the experience of a subscriber, one Ms. O. (a typical San Francisco mother).

The precipitating cause for the entire event was the occurrence of a febrile convulsion which caused her three-year-old son to roll his eyes back in his head so only the whites showed, and go into a seizure. According to the paper, her son's fever was about 105 degrees. He went into convulsions. The subjective experience of a patient in a febrile convulsion has been described to me by a young epileptic. Imagine the pure energy space of Mr. Sollo while the body thrashes around. Every convulsive movement of the body is felt as a surge in the intensity of pure radiant energy. Time and space disappear just like when you flip a TV tuner to another channel. The treatment for high-fever convulsions is simple; bring the temperature down as quickly as possible by any means at hand.

I used to advise my patients to strip the child and dunk the entire body into a bath of tepid water. In most cases it is enough to merely remove all the layers of clothes and blankets. Allow the body to cool, the temperature drops, and the convulsions stop. Keep this simple procedure in mind as our saga continues. This procedure, combined with the administration of common baby aspirin, will alleviate and prevent the recurrence of the vast majority of fever convulsions. It certainly would have stopped the one being described.

Over a three-hour period, the mother kept calling the doctor assigned to her. She got no answer. Ms. O. then called one general hospital and then another. Finally she found one that would accept her PHP card. They wouldn't treat the child without authorization from her doctor who wasn't answering his telephone that day. The child went into another convulsive seizure while she was trying to reach an emergency number which nobody answered. At this point Ms. O. (a typical mother) simply went to pieces, "began weeping and begging the hospital personnel to treat her son." She was told to take him to another hospital. She didn't have any money with her, she belonged to a prepaid health plan and she had her card. Somebody called the police. The police drove the patient and his mother to yet another hospital where "they persuaded the doctors to help." At that point I suppose someone took off his clothes, sponged him with alcohol, gave him three baby aspirins and put him to bed.

"Do you suppose Ms. O. made the whole thing up? Or maybe the kid made it up, eh?" Abbie is home from school. It's a holiday. "Maybe you made up the newspaper."

"Then who's making me up?"

The starship "Enterprise" materializes on the TV screen. A program called "Star Trek" is in progress—the spaceship's captain is speaking. "Those life forms up there in the flying saucers. They are projecting a three-dimensional color hologram all around creating the illusion in your mind that you live in a physical body on a planet containing a multiplicity of life forms. They make the seasons, they make it rain, they provide the sun. They project three-dimensional space and time, then they immerse their consciousness in it and try to take it over by force."

"Oh boy! Life entities out there in space dreaming us. When we fall asleep we die to the time and space world and wake up on the flying saucer . . . or in the pure energy field," says fourteen-year-old Ben.

The telephone bell rings. The little plastic voice in my head is calling me. It sounds terrible; it says it has been in bed for two weeks because of back pain. Like the entities in space, I project a hologram with my mind. With my mind's eye, I see a young man from Massachusetts, in pajamas and robe, lying in bed, chain smoking. He is holding a plastic object in his hand as I am, only his is a *red* plastic voice-in-the-head-maker. The young man, as I see him in my mind's eye, is talking into *his* telephone to a voice in *his* head which he thinks is *me*. He is simultaneously projecting a hologram with his mind to provide the little voice in his head with a three-dimensional imaginary body. He and I are a pair of holograms simultaneously making each other up!

"I belong to a Prepaid Health Plan. They're treating me for a bad back. They gave me some tranquilizers and told me to stay in bed for three weeks. It's been raining all that time. I heard that there is some kind of sound machine around that could fix my back, and that you had one."

Like *Grandpoppa* (the hologram in Susan's head), *Bill*, the hologram in my head, is autonomous. In spite of the fact that I made it up in my mind, it acts independently of me, and I have no idea what it will do next. When Susan first saw Grandpoppa she was advised to treat him as if he were real, conduct herself courteously, and assume that he meant her no harm. I can do no less for my own holograms. I can perhaps add the assumption that they are trying to teach me something. On the basis of this last assumption, I chatted with Bill about the recently completed four-year Headlands experiment. He seemed interested, so we agreed to materialize each other in time and space; the green plastic voice then gave me an address on Russian Hill in San Francisco. The materialization will take place at that point on the planet Earth at one o'clock in the afternoon, two days hence. "I have a psychiatrist's appointment at eleven. I'd drag myself there if I had to go through hell and high water." At this point the rain stops and the sun begins to shine brightly.

Two days later, I find myself at the appointed time and place. Bill materializes as a thin, tallish young man living alone in a bachelor apartment. He is not confined to bed, he walks without a limp, he chain smokes, and his telephone is blue. It differs from mine in that it has push buttons instead of a circular dial. His attending Health Plan physician has given him some muscle relaxant pills, a bottle of tranquilizer tablets, and instructions to remain in bed. He has just returned from a visit to his psychiatrist, having ignored the instructions of the PHP doctor. He did not find there what he was seeking.

"Relief of pain in my back, and something to calm me down. My nerves are shot . . . Those psychiatrists, they're all full of shit. Every last one of 'em I've been to has been full of shit!" He is interested in electronics and can go along with the idea that a one-megacycle beam of vibratory energy administered into points of decreased electrical resistance on his skin might redirect his flow of body energies and make him feel better. He is able to imagine himself in "a blue energy field." He can't visualize someone in the field while he circulates his body energy during the sound application. He said the treatment made him feel much better. He felt pleasantly stoned, and thought that was due to thirty minutes of hyperventilation. He really likes being on our planet, and would like to get back to "bopping around North Beach."

When I suggest that perhaps he is overamping the body he's in, he agrees, "I guess this backache is trying to keep me out of trouble. Do you think you could write me for some downers? Tuinal, Quaalude, Valium—anything that'll quiet my nerves."

I remind him of my Hippocratic physician's oath in which I agreed to "administer no poisons even though I am requested to do so."

He complains that his time/space body seems to have a mind of its own; "I'll just have to accept its limitations. I don't seem to have any choice." We agree that he will try to control his physical and emotional difficulties by circulating the energy composing his physical body for fifteen minutes three times a day until he and the body come to terms and the symptoms abate. As part of a ritual of departure, I write the meditation instructions on a prescription blank, tear off the sheet, and solemnly hand it to my materialized hologram. In return, he hands me a twenty dollar bill and three fives as I walk out the door.

The Dream

I am sitting on the porch overlooking the magnificent bay. In the distance I can see San Francisco glowing brilliant white in the afternoon sun. It looks like a mythical city called "Camelot." The head of the psychedelically colored bay butts up against a high mountain. The mountain, after ten days of rain, is glowing an emerald green which reflects off a layer of fleecy white clouds in a fantastically blue sky. I look at all this and decide "This must be heaven!"

Marty the medical director drives up in a brand new white Porsche. He is working in an emergency room in a hospital up north. Still dedicated to the original idea of research into the essence of the healing process, he is negotiating with the acupuncture department of the U. C. Medical School in San Francisco. He wants to set up a study to determine the efficacy of sonopuncture compared with that of standard twentieth century techniques currently employed in their out- patient clinics. He feels that if he can verify the results we were getting with Applied Alchemy at our own clinic, the technique will be quickly accepted by physicians around the world. It is in this way that he can contribute to the alleviation of human suffering while he continues to explore the delicious mystery of the relations between the sexes.

Returning to my bedroom, I close my eyes, relax my body and idly direct my attention to the images floating through my mind. A woman, named Isis, dressed in black appears for a moment. She is smoking a joint and gives it to me. I take a puff and return it to her, whereupon she puffs deeply on the grass, bursts into laughter which sounds like a running brook and points to a nearby redwood tree. As I observe these events running through my consciousness, the thought occurs to me that this whole thing is a dream.

A young man, about twenty-five steps out through an opening in the tree. He explains patiently, "That Director of the Headlands Clinic, your hologram, is the guy who was watching TV with a bunch of teenagers in your last scene. "I'm really much older," he explains, "but I'm projecting myself to you as a twenty-five-year-old." He further explains to me that the thoughts which I have been watching are setting the pattern for my experiences down there in the space/time continuum we have been calling "the planet Earth."

"If this a dream," I think, it must be happening for a reason." I assume that its purpose is to give me some sort of a message. I will observe and record the events as I experience them, and watch for the message. The young man, dressed in blue, tells me he is going to instruct me in "How to Control Your Hologram—A Study in Magic." He says that he has been hanging around the twilight zone for years trying to explain to the people how to create and control their holograms. "They just keep smashing up one after the other." He explains that if more people knew how the hologram worked, they wouldn't have so much trouble. "We project a beam of quarks down onto the planet. Those quarks arrange themselves into the matter of the hologram duplicating the pattern you set with your mind."

An old man with a gray beard saunters up and makes himself comfortable. "It's sort of a rest and recreation program." He enlightens me to the fact that we are located on a spaceship which has been traveling around for four and a half billion years. Everyone aboard had forgotten the original purpose of the space voyage. They were now experimenting with a new method of entertainment for those who were "tired of hanging out in the white light chamber meditating."

"It's really very simple," says the old man. "It works just like a remote control tuner; change the rate of vibrations you emit from your cerebral cortex and you change the channel." He describes an ingenious system by means of which the mind of the space voyager can enjoy an interminable voyage.

"Just like the movies on the long airplane flights?"

"Precisely."

"We train the mind to concentrate a beam of quarks exactly on the optic chiasm. The space through which we are traveling contains a limitless supply of quarks easily available to the mind wishing to tap into it. The quarks have certain characteristics of their own. If the mind inhabiting the hologram ignores these characteristics, the hologram begins to disintegrate in a most painful manner."

"The science of controlling the hologram is called magic," says the young man in blue. He says he is a scientist researching practical cabbalism for his doctoral dissertation.

"The quarks basic characteristic is motion in a spiral; the path of a snake is an example of this characteristic behavior of our prima materia. We can determine the sex or polarity of a quark by its manifested behavior. We have no means of demonstrating them to the mind, except for their behavior visualized holographically. They display a mating tendency which is insatiable and infinitely intense. The males usually travel in groups of three, and the females in groups of four. When you project into your holographic android down there in time/space remember this characteristic. This information will serve you in good stead."

"The key lies in conscious attention," says the old man, whose name is Albert Karl. *"Focus your total conscious attention on your optic chiasm. Your face is about one square foot; focus on an area about one cubic inch back from the skin between your eyes. Focus your total attention on the light impulses from each eye. Find the point where they meet and concentrate on that."* He explains that the procedure allows quarks to enter consciousness in groups of four. *"Arrange groups of four quarks along a double spiral and you have a perfect model of the DNA chain which uses*

four molecules, carbon, nitrogen, hydrogen and oxygen to create the time and space form of any offspring." He's talking about genes which guide the developing embryo into its proper form—dog, bird, human or worm. "The geneticists' big mistake was that they thought that this system only operated at the level of the gene."

He ventures the opinion that the reason it takes four molecules to make genes is that everything is made of quarks. "Four quarks can store all the information necessary to create an entire space/time hologram (you call it a creature). Concentrate your attention and they (the quarks) spiral along the optic nerves, producing the sensation of pure light or pure energy. If you like, we have teaching machines which will help you concentrate them in the correct area."

The conversation continues in this vein, becoming increasingly more complex and esoteric. I gather that I am to structure my hologram by creating a word picture in my mind in the same manner by which I created Bill (adding a mental image to the voice vibrating in my head through the telephone).

A small book called Rules of the Game Book *appears on the table before me. It says that I must endow my character with four facets. It is best if I can conceive of one description which combines three other aspects. I decide that I would like to be a retired physician who is manifesting as an author, lecturer and world traveler. Albert Karl suggests that it is important for me to remember my purpose in making this venture into time and space. He thinks it would be nice if I could achieve wholeness (health), manifesting as contentment, fulfillment and enlightenment. "Your purpose on what you call the physical plane is to understand and master it. This is achieved by avoiding goal-directed activity."*

My physical form will be created by my own self-image. A characteristic of all holograms is their temporal instability. I am warned to remember at all times that time/space events are transient and constantly changing. This is because quarks create the hologram by means of continuously flowing through the mind in a perpetual flux of constantly changing patterns. Thoughts and mental images shape the flow pat-

terns which then crystallize into what we call matter. The world is crystallized thought!

"It has to be reprogrammed continuously," says the little red book. "It is possible for the mind to become imprisoned in the hologram if it forgets the creative role of thought and visual imagery. This can be a catastrophic experience for the untrained mind." It is like being trapped in a 3D horror movie because you forgot where the exits are. *"This unfortunate complication can be avoided if the traveler through the space/time continuum learns to stop thinking at will."*

"The plastic malleable substance of the quark can be galvanized into activity by a trained will and imagination," says the book. "Its substance is particularly susceptible to the working of the imagination which possesses the power to transform its perpetual flux and shapelessness into molds and matrices which the will can stabilize and energize powerfully in a given direction." "What that means," says the young man, "is that quarks are very impressionable. This is because of their habit of going on and off constantly. I have theorized that they oscillate back and forth through little black holes in space to and from an anti-quark universe (or a meta quark universe . . .). Just like we oscillate between the space platform (the twilight zone) and the time/space continuum (the planet earth)."

My mind begins to form a picture of a stream of quarks oscillating between the planet Earth and the space platform, creating each alternately. "That android down there on the planet creates you with his thoughts just as you are now creating him with yours. We do it just for fun, rest and recreation."

"If you're doing it just for fun," I ask, "whence all the pain and suffering that goes on down there?"

"The chief cause for suffering is ignorance," murmurs Albert Karl who has turned into an old Chinese gentleman named Lao Tzu. "My old friend, Chuang, thought that he really was a butterfly. He would go to sleep convinced that he turned into the butterfly flying about in his dreams. He awoke every morning certain that the butterfly was sleeping *and dreaming him. One day," continues Lao Tzu, "he didn't wake up. Do you suppose he went back to being a butterfly full time?"*

"We have many passengers aboard who spend all their time in the white light chamber contemplating their navels. They never transport down to any planet."

"Those who enter the white light never return," says the old Chinese gentleman. He says that I might consider spending the rest of our endless journey in a weightless condition without a body bathed in an ecstatically delicious stream of congruent quark energy.

"I'm still having a pretty good time down there," I reply. "I don't feel quite ready to give it up before I've carried out the author-lecturer and world traveler scenario."

"Suit yourself," he says taking off his long robe to reveal Albert Karl's brown suit with a large silver watch chain running from one vest pocket to disappear into another. He looks like the rabbit from Alice in Wonderland. *"Your subjective experience depends on the number of quarks which pass through your mind each second. If you pass them through your attention filter in groups of thirteen or more, you will experience them as thoughts. Groups of twenty-four per second arrange themselves in a pattern we call the planet and all its life forms . . . material reality." The young scientist interjects, "That's what you call the beta state. If you narrow the attention filter to admit groups smaller than thirteen, but larger than seven, you receive only uniform colored light into your consciousness. That's what old Lao here means when he says, 'when thoughts cease phenomena cease.' The old man nods his agreement. "That's alpha."*

"Whenever I beam down to the planet I run my mind at a rate which keeps me sort of midway down. I call the place space station Nirvana. I set my android on automatic and let my mind drift back out into space. There are some passengers who have spent several thousand Earth years spaced out on Nirvana. To get there all you have to do is to shift your mind oscillator into the alpha range. The quarks do the rest automatically." The old man continues to

oscillate between Lao Tzu and Albert Karl switching from one form to the other about ten times per second. "The trick is to find the razor's edge in your mind where the two fuse, then you are simultaneously both and neither. You are who you really are. Fix your attention on the light entering your eye from each figure. It is actually a double alternating stroboscope emiting quantum bursts of quarks in groups of ten or multiples of ten for each light flash. This fascinating machine was invented by Isis." As he says this I catch a glimpse of her still in the black dress, blowing smoke in my direction, and giggling uncontrollably.

My young instructor tells me to follow the spiraling double helix of quark packets back along my optic nerves to the point where they meet. "I only see two lights flashing on and off alternately like at a railroad crossing."

"That's them. You're doing fine." I feel an encouraging pat on my shoulder. If you watch carefully, you will note that they meet at your optic chiasm . . . where the nerves cross . . . about one inch back from the center of your forehead. Follow the homing device. You will hear a musical note when you are on course. Make course adjustments necessary to keep it strong and clear." Soon I am aware of nothing but the lights flashing in a steady ten cycles-persecond rhythm. The musical note in my ear is beautiful, loud, and clear. A pulsating violet light fills my consciousness. "We can change the color by lowering the rate of vibration between the two poles. That takes us stepwise down the spectrum to red."

I remember that point from my high school physics, and the musical tone stops abruptly. "You shifted into beta with the thought. That happens as soon as your attention wanders from the light. Watch closely now, I am about to shift down into delta." As the light flashes decrease their frequency, I become more and more aware of the utter blackness which separates the two flashing poles. The light suffusing my visual field changes color slowly, becomes grey and less frequent until at one point it remains in the "off" position. There is only the black in between the light flashes. "We

*have arrived at the delta range." Inside black nothing! "You
are simultaneously awake and asleep yet neither. You are
who you really are."*

*My instructor then tells me that he is going to slowly in-
crease his vibratory rate from four to twenty-four cycles per
second. I am to carefully note that the frequency range I experience is the total range of planetary consciousness.*

"It's really quite extensive, as you shall see."

*Absolute blackness fuses with absolute silence. I am exper-
iencing total sensory deprivation! "Watch those thoughts,"
occurs to me against the silent black background which is in-
termittently pierced by the pulsating grey light. Four pulsa-
tions per second.*

*"A border," says the instructor. "Now entering theta and
leaving delta." Suddenly I am at the San Francisco Airport
waiting for a plane. I walk to the boarding area alone. I realize I have no tickets. The thirty-five dollars I got from Bill
for the treatment is also gone. I board a commercial aircraft;
the stewardess tells me that I have already handed in my
boarding pass, and that I am to occupy seat #6 up front for
our flight to London. I am only vaguely aware of the blackness between the pulses as my instructor vibrates at six cycles
per second. Isis is seated beside me in seat #7 on the flight.
We chat amiably as we travel through space. We seem to
have become traveling companions.*

*She comments, "Did you know that 1975 is International
Women's Year?" Her name is no longer Isis but she offers
no substitute. I realize that I never asked her what she would
like to be called. Another shift in scene, and I am on a city
street which appears to be partly dug up. A red double
decker bus works its way around an obstruction and I realize, "It's London all right." I am standing on the edge of a
sheer precipice. Dropping to my stomach, I crawl to the edge
and peer down to the lower level far below. I am on a stage
with a group of performers. Leading down is the flat side of
a huge redwood log which is used by the entertainers for their
descent. Grabbing a guide rope, I slide over the edge. The
descent takes me through a pure colored energy field. I am*

relieved that the wood contains no splinters as I flash on the thought that I am performing in a play within a dream. The energy field is marked at both ends of the slide by a border according to my instructor, who is now vibrating at thirteen cycles per second the beta range. I become aware of strong sunlight streaming in my window; get out of bed, and brush my teeth while trying to piece together the parts of the dream I have just completed. I think, "Perhaps I'd better write all this down." As you can see, I did.

Out on the front porch, my teenagers are having breakfast. Kathy and Keith, a young couple from London, have stopped over on their first visit to America. Suddenly Kathy begins giggling uncontrollably. They are listening to a local rock FM station which is yelling, "The British are coming! The British are coming!"

They've been sitting around discussing a *National Geographic* article on Jupiter, called "Mystery Surrounds the Biggest Planet."

"Did you know," says Keith, "that Jupiter is so huge that it alone makes up nearly three-quarters of the entire mass of all the planets and moons in the whole solar system?"

"That's the planet the Greeks and Romans personified as the god Zeus or Jove. He's the old guy who's always hurling thunderbolts at the Earth," says Fred. "Their scientists must have known about those wild radio storms." He reads from the article: "(They) last for several minutes at a time. By one calculation they equal the energy of two one megaton hydrogen bomb explosions per second."

"What's the old boy's power source?"

"Unknown at present. He radiates almost two and a half times as much energy as he receives from the sun." Keith notes that the Jovian atmosphere contains the building blocks which we think created life on the planet Earth.

"I bet you could create a viable scientific hypothesis to

suggest that Jupiter is actually a living creature,'' Fred continues his speculations. "We know that all serious scientists now agree that extra-terrestrial life forms exist, probably in our galaxy as in others." Warming up to his topic, he suggests that there is not one shred of evidence coming back from the Pioneer space probes which would cast doubt on the validity of his hypothesis. "On the other hand, look at the evidence in support of it." He reads the words of one Dr. Cecil Ponnamperuma, director of the Laboratory of Chemical Evolution of the University of Maryland. "We've taken the Jovian atmosphere and applied lightning to it. Other forms of energy such as ultraviolet radiation will work as well. The result is an organic polymer known as nitrile. Combine nitrile with water and we get amino acids—the building blocks of proteins and thus of all life: from the smallest microbe to the largest creature."

"By Jove!" says Keith. (He sounds like Ringo Starr.)

"Experiments like this convince me," continues Dr. Ponnamperuma, "that life could evolve on Jupiter and, indeed, already has done so. It is perhaps unreasonable to believe that life could exist only on one planet." Ben points out that Jupiter is not solid like the Earth. "It is composed entirely of hydrogen-helium gas compressed down to a liquid slush. And what, may you ask, is in that slush?" demands Abbie. Fred strikes a stance with his right finger pointing up to the sky as he reads the word from the book cradled in his left palm. The word is that of Dr. Robert S. Lewis of the Massachusetts Institute of Technology, "whose concept of the Jovian atmosphere is widely accepted." He says, "For those who look for life on Jupiter, the water clouds form the most important part of the planet. Here is abundant water, an invariable requirement for any forms of life we know. And here are hydrogen, methane, and ammonia—prime ingredients of the primordial soup in which, many scientists believe, life on Earth originated billions of years ago." Ben suggests that the great red spot in the southern hemisphere could be the creature's eye. Fred reads again from the article:

"For more than three hundred years, astronomers have

observed this baleful Cyclopean eye; never dreaming that it was staring right back at them." The girls giggle. The anatomy lesson continues. "17,000 miles long by 8,500 miles wide, it drifts slowly around the planet. Its length fluctuates, its color waxes and wanes, but even when the red has faded to grey, it is still visible."

"Sleeping, I suppose," snorts Abbie.

"It rotates counterclockwise, once every twelve Earth days." Fred conjectures that the thought must also have occurred to the NASA scientists. "I'll bet that's why they put that plaque on the outside hull of Pioneer 10!" He reads the description of the plaque sent out from Earth to Jupiter on the December 1973 flyby. There is a diagram of the hydrogen atom, the most common element in the universe. Radiating lines give the bearings from our sun to 14 pulsars. Human figures in front show how big we are and what we look like. A map of our solar system indicates Pioneer's track from Earth out past Jupiter.

"It all adds up to a message to intelligent beings," says the *National Geographic* Magazine (February 1975, p· 294). "You are not alone."

"Wasn't Arthur C. Clarke's movie, *2001, A Space Odyssey,* about a trip to Jupiter?"

"Shit! my contact lens is cracked. I knew it would be cracked—I just knew when I put it away something was going to happen to it. Would it be bad if I wore only the left lens for a while? I'm right eyed."

"Why do you wear lenses at all?"

"I want to see clearly, stupid." Kathy likes to see things the way they really are so she won't walk into telephone poles and the like. If she wears only one corrective lens, she will see a double image for a while. Eventually her mind will make the adjustment so she will once again create a clear, hard edged impression of her environment.

"The fact is, that with or without your brand new contact lenses you see the world upside down and backwards. You can get glasses which let you see the world like it really is, only then it looks upside down and backwards. You're actually standing with your feet up on the ground and your head pointed down at the sky."

"Oh yeah, what keeps me from falling off, dummy?"

"Gravity, my girl, gravity. Nearsighted people have a distinct advantage in not being quite sure how the world really looks. Without my glasses, I see four full moons with blurry edges. Put them on, and I see a white circle with sharp edges; maybe even a face. Add binoculars, and I see craters with radiating lines on a huge white ball. On the TV screen it looks like a Star Trek set."

Kathy remembers the experiment. "When they wore those glasses for a week, everything looked normal. Then when they took them off, everything looked upside down and backwards."

"Which is normal!" A red Fiat sports convertible pulls up and Marty the Medical Director joins the group. He says he is about to turn thirty. "Looks like my adolescence is coming to an end." He considers it within the realm of possibility that Jupiter is a giant living creature. "A mind-blowing idea, but entirely possible." He is just back from Los Angeles where he has been playing the part of team doctor for the Commander Cody rock band. "I drove to L. A. and then we were up all night.

"The next thing I knew, I was back in my room. I had fallen asleep standing up with all my clothes on! I went right over to UCLA because I was late for an appointment. When I got there, I told the guy what had happened and said I had to meditate for a half hour in order to get myself together. I had barely closed my eyes in the next room when I was in front of the great wall of China. Right in front of me was a tower made of pure ivory—an ivory tower. A second later I was in the same place only it was several thousand years later at an archeological dig site. The tower was all crumbled and broken. Right after that I felt completely rested and refreshed. I've never had such an experience before."

Closing my eyes, I relax and let my mind drift away from the scene. "Do you know the Tarot card called "The Blasted

*Tower?'' I realize that I am back in theta. With a start I real-
ize that I am also back on the space platform. Albert Karl
appears wearing a floor length shiny black coat with a fur
hat. Beside him is a huge Tarot card; one foot wide by six
feet tall, depicting a tower like the one Marty the Medical Director has just described. A bolt of lightning is striking the
top, knocking a huge crown from the battlements. Falling
along with the crown are a man and a woman. Flames erupt
from the top and surround the falling pair. "It is interesting
to note that when lightning flashes were photographed at the
Westinghouse Laboratories, they were shown to be spirals,
rather than zigzags. Old Jupiter pitches only screw-balls."*

*"In terms of consciousness," continues the old man, "the
lightning flash which originates in the Jovian energy storm,
symbolizes a sudden, momentary glimpse of the truth. Zeus'
thunderbolt completely upsets all our old notions. The
blasted tower symbolizes the destruction of Marty's whole
former philosophy regarding constitution of reality."*

*"The truth is," says a voice in my head, "that the planet
Earth and all the life forms on it, exist on the back of your
eyeballs. Would you like to watch the NBC Evening News?"*

*John Chancellor introduces a story about a fire in a New
York skyscraper housing telephone equipment. "170,000
New Yorkers awoke this morning to find it was no ordinary
fire . . . 24,000 phones will be out for six to eight weeks. It is
the worst fire in the history of the telephone company." A
21-inch color television set has appeared in the window of a
lower story of the burning, lightning-struck tower. The tube
is showing a picture of another burning, destroyed tower.
For good measure, the commercial break includes a pitch for
a movie called* The Towering Inferno, *with more photos of
burning towers.*

*"When a paradigm collapses, the entire society 't creates
collapses along with it," says the voice in my head as the
newscast describes worldwide depression, war, and general-
ized chaos. Every forecast is that things are going to get
much worse. Food riots, mass starvation, and brutal government repression are on the immediate horizon." A pic-*

ture of a hippy general practitioner fills the screen. Curly black hair spirals out in all directions, surrounding his face. He looks a bit like Rasputin the mad monk, and declares himself to be a disciple of Albert Einstein. "I expect that within six months, we will be living under a right or left wing dictatorship." It is his intention to move his family to an area of relative safety and freedom inaccessible to any governmental agency. He feels that his type of early twentieth century allopathic medicine is still desperately needed by the community, and would like another physician to pick up the torch so to speak. "I'd like someone to practice like I do; take emergencies, do some minor office surgery, and handle general stuff like pneumonia, flu, backaches, and such."

Realizing the futility of his search for a replacement he makes an attempt to soften the blow. "I think the most important thing I did for people was to provide a place where they could come in out of the storm, relax, smoke a joint, and talk about healing. I think my patients would have gotten well no matter what I did." He illustrates this point with a story; "My brother-in-law called me over last week to treat a sore throat for him. He thinks I'm a crazy hippy, but he's impressed by the fact that I can write prescriptions. I gave him an ampicillin capsule. Two minutes after he swallowed it, he was sighing with relief and telling me what a great doctor I am. I knew damned well that the capsule hadn't even dissolved in his stomach yet!" He fades out with a quizzical expression on his face.

"This chaos we are watching," says my guide, "is the state in which the opposites are at war. There are two basic oppositions operating on the planet. First, there is the war between the men and the women (more about that later). Secondly, there is the conflict between those who believe in magic and those who don't. These two conflicts have occupied humanity since the beginning of conscious thought. An illustration follows:"

The TV screen is filled with a photo of the San Francisco Chronicle *dated March 1, 1975. (My instructor tells me to pay careful attention to this part, because it contains the key to understanding and enjoying my hologram.) Page 7 is discussing "A Plan to Examine Practitioners of the Occult" in an article entitled "LICENSING OF ASTROLOGERS—A GALAXY OF OPINION." A male against magic identifies himself as a firm believer in the laws of cause and effect. His name is Dan. He has been teaching courses on astrology at various colleges for the past five years. He is currently engaged in researching the correlation between horoscopes and "personality tests used by psychologists."*

I wonder if he's trying to show that the astrologers are right because the psychologists say so, or vice versa. My instructor notes that the psychologists, like all humans are divided into male and female, each of those groups consisting of believers in magic vs. believers in cause and effect. "If you understand this quaternity, you understand the secret of Jupiter," he says.

"If one is using only astrology and not consulting techniques on personality, then one is a fortune teller," says Dan to a mixture of applause and groans. His opposite pole is played by "a woman known only as Grace." She objects to government attempting to interfere in a sacred science. "Grace is the archetypal female for magic," says the voice in my head. "The next item will define the transsexual aspect of the primal conflict more explicity."

The next item on the news broadcast concerns the paradigm clash which currently churns up the fields of psychology and psychiatry. In this example, both protagonists are male. Piaget, a noted psychologist, poses the question, "What turns a helpless infant into a reasoning adult?"

"The same thing that turns an egg into a chicken," giggles Grace.

"Only man," observes the eminent man, "can contemplate and then theorize."

"Male chauvinist pig!" observes Grace, no longer giggling.

When Piaget makes the statement that "Object permanence is the foundation for symbolic thought," she shouts, "There! That's the key to the whole thing! He thinks chil-

dren convert a real *world into pictures or into thoughts inside
their heads. He presumes that mere things have a life of their
own."*

*"The ability to transform an object into a thought is some-
thing that simply develops . . . like the ability to walk.*

"At first," says Dan, *"the child cannot distinguish between the object and the thought. Later, he cannot distinguish between his thoughts and those of the other people in
his environment." Grace mutters that this common problem
rarely disappears with the passing of childhood.*

*"Professor Piaget, as you can see, represents the attitude
of a male who takes a position midway between belief in
magic, and faith in the laws of cause and effect. He says that
the ability to think appears spontaneously, by magic so to
speak. His postulates that objects become thoughts, but he
says nothing about* thoughts becoming objects. *Anyway,
how can you have a permanent object in a world made of
quarks which are constantly going on and off? She explains
that the opposite poles of the paradigm clash within psychiatry and psychology is represented by a cause-and-effect fanatic named Skinner. "The behaviorist position is that even
proper thinking is a thing that must be taught."*

"Development," says Dr. Skinner on the TV screen,
*"depends completely on learning. It is not something that
just grows. We must* teach *basic concepts. It is* not *enough to
provide a full environment. First, you understand basic concepts,* then *you experiment!"*

"Look," exclaims Grace. *"He looks exactly like that gen-
eticist Popov; the one who died in chains in Russia on that TV
program down there."*

*The only chain binding him, is the chain of cause and ef-
fect.*

"You must have dozed off in the sun." The voice is
Marty's. I am back on the front porch in the beta range in-
trigued by the idea that I might actually be experiencing a
hologram of my own creation.

The Hologram

The calendar says March 3, 1975; the clock on the wall says 5:12. The *I Ching* discusses the current apocalypse represented by the blasted tower symbol. The hexagram for this balmy springlike day is #42: *Increase*.

"The fact that continuous decrease finally leads to a change into its opposite, increase, lies in the course of nature, as can be perceived in the waning and waxing of the moon and in all of the regularly recurring processes of nature." The cyclic waves of apocalypse and renaissance follow each other like ocean tides. Since anything pushed to its extreme turns into its opposite, it is safe to assume that when things get this bad, they must inevitably improve. Seasonal change is another example from nature which illustrates that vital principle governing all human and other natural affairs. Winter and summer, fall and spring, are two pair of opposites comprising the totality of the year. They follow each other in a cyclic pattern which has nothing at all to do with cause and effect.

"It's like day and night," says fourteen-year-old Ben as he ties his shoelaces. "One turns into the other all the time, but that doesn't mean that one makes the other."

Abbie, his twin sister is extremely skeptical. "That's a lot of baloney! I think nothing ever happens unless something makes it happen."

"Oh yeah? Then what makes deaf people hear music, wise guy?"

"Ben, you're such a jerk it's pathetic. How can someone who is supposed to be deaf hear anything?"

Triumphantly, Ben produces the morning paper. Page four carries an article entitled, "Auditory Hallucinations—Music that only the deaf can hear." It seems that deaf people hear very clearly, according to a report taken from the *Journal of the American Medical Association.*

"Three big shot neurologists from Boston are reporting about this eighty-year-old guy who has been deaf for ten years and came to the doctor complaining that he can hear rock and roll music, Irish Jigs, and Christmas carols. A seventy-year-old man, deaf as a stone, heard hymns and church bells in his head. He reads, "Doctors assured them that deaf people sometimes experience auditory hallucinations, and that their symptoms were not a sign that they were insane."

"I'll bet that made them feel better," Abbie chuckles. "How did they finally get rid of the symptoms?" A dedicated cause and effect disciple, she wants to know what *caused* the phantom hymns, church bells, and Christmas carols.

"Why would a deaf guy want to get rid of the sound of music in his head?" Ben is delighted at the chance to needle her.

"Because it's not normal, that's why!" Ben's opposite twin shows signs of successful needling. He reads on: "The hallucinations usually began acutely in the deaf or deafer ear after a long history of progressive hearing loss. The music was a highly organized, vivid, and intricate perception."

Abbie asserts that anyone who hears bells which aren't there is crazy as far as she is concerned.

Her opinion is apparently shared by most American physicians as well as by most recipients of the questionable blessing. The article continues, "Most American doctors have come to consider auditory hallucinations as symptoms of epilepsy, brain tumors, brain damage from chronic alcoholism, and mental disorders such as psychoses and schizophrenia." The National Center for Health Statistics says that al-

most four million Americans have hearing problems. Just
how many are subject to the problem of auditory hallucinations is unknown.

Abbie comments, "If I was deaf and started to hear bells,
music and voices, I sure as hell wouldn't tell anyone. I'd
wind up on some funny farm in five minutes."

The newspaper report agrees, "Just how many of these
four million have auditory hallucinations is unknown, but
the incidence may well be more common than is generally
appreciated, since patients may not seek medical attention or
may be reluctant to mention the symptom for fear that it
would suggest a psychiatric disorder."

"How do they decide who's crazy and who's normal, if all
those people are hearing things which aren't there?"

"The authors, Drs. Elliot D. Ross, Paul B. Jossman, Ben
Bell, Thomas Sabin and Norman Geshwind of Harvard,
Boston University, and Tufts Medical School suggested that
some deaf patients who described hallucinations might be
mistakenly referred to psychiatrists or hospitalized in psychiatric wards" (for the rest of their natural lives!). The doctors' report was designed to alert more doctors to the
little appreciated normal phenomenon, and to prevent the
occurrence of some real personal tragedies. "In contrast to
'psychotics' who did not realize that their hallucinations
were not real, the deaf patients fully appreciated that what
they were hearing did not exist outside of the mind."

We're not sure when someone is definitely dead; now it's
not clear which definition of crazy is accurate. As these
thoughts cross my mind, the room and the pair of quarreling
opposites (the twins) seems to become less distinct as my
mind shifts from 24 to 13 cycles per second. I realize that I
am fully awake. "This," I think, "must be the hologram on
the planet!"

*Trying out the controls, so to speak, I find that I can easily
shift my attention from my environment to my thoughts at
will. The thoughts in my head and the fascinating activities
of the twins in my living room compete for my attention.*

"We are the same." Closing my eyes, I see a young boy in

an orange and white striped beret topped with a white pom-pom.

I must have dropped below seven cycles per second into theta range. Closing my eyes, and breathing slowly I can make thoughts and images stop. That lets me know that I am operating my mind in the alpha range. I am certain that with a little practice I can avoid being trapped in a three-dimensional color horror movie with quadraphonic sound. This disaster can befall me only if I forget to go through all four mental gears in a cyclic and orderly manner. The imaginary six-year-old boy in the beret with the pom-pom, has folded his arms behind his back as his spread-eagled feet skate around in a circle. He suggests that the flow of the four seasons is a good guide. He says he would like to be called "Theta" (the yiddish word for grandpoppa*). He informs me that from this point on, I am on my own. Anytime I feel like, I can shift down into theta and materialize him on my optic chiasm. He and his friends will guide me from there. Before speeding off on a motorcycle, he tells me he only shows up when he feels like it. "Check #31 in the* I *Ching," he calls over his shoulder as he disappears.*

On page 131 of my copy of the Wilhelm translation, I find the hexagram #31 called *influence*. It appears to be a treatise on how to manage my hologram. The relevant passage catches my eye at once.

"What takes place in the depths of one's being, in the unconscious mind can neither be called forth nor prevented by the conscious mind." Theta, a product of my subconscious mind comes and goes as he pleases. The events which transpire on my optic chiasm, which is in the depths of my being (my skull), are autonomous. That idea seems to ring a bell . . .

The telephone bell rings at that precise moment. A voice says it is a woman reporter named Ms. Pixie. She would like to interview me as a participant in a conference on healing coming up at University of California, Santa Cruz, this month. "I like the girl who is running it, and I'd like to give her some publicity," she says. I realize at once that the last time I heard that voice, it was saying that 1975 is International Women's Year. That can only mean one thing. Isis, my female traveling companion is about to join me down here in time/space! As in that first materialization involving Bill, I am given an address in San Francisco, and told to appear at eleven o'clock in the morning six days hence. The interview and the materialization will take place together.

"Who was that?" Abbie wants to know.

"The High Priestess," I reply mysteriously.

"Really? I didn't know you were involved with a lady priest," she laughs and scampers out the door followed by her opposite twin. This action causes me to muse, "Ms. Pixie, what a great name she chose. She really has a sense of humor." Ms. Pixie and I are, like Bill and I were, a pair of holograms making each other up!

Of course! It's obvious! I realize any holographic person which I make up has got to be my opposite in some way. Ms. Pixie (I really like that name) is of the opposite sex. (Bill played patient which is the opposite of my role as doctor.)

As I ponder thus on the problem of the opposites, I close my eyes for a moment and breathe regularly, thinking of nothing in particular.

Suddenly the old man appears on my optic chiasm and poses a riddle:

"What is it that you do not understand and can only be expressed in unfathomable paradoxes?" A sense of relief and gratitude floods my being as I realize that I am still receiving guidance in this new experience, "The most formidable opposition," he explains, "is the relationship between the male and the female. We are inclined to think of this primarily as the power of love, of passion, which drives the two opposite poles together, forgetting that such a vehement attraction is needed only when an equally strong resistance keeps them apart. Man and woman are natural, primal, enemies."

As if to punctuate the message, Abbie suddenly runs back into the house, slamming the door behind her in a fury. "I hate all males!" she shouts, "Especially that asshole Ben!" Throwing the morning paper at my head she disappears into her room in a flurry of slamming doors and reverberating walls.

FURIOUS MINISTERS SMITE SMUT SHOP, screams the headline on page three, perpetuating the mood as it discusses an incident involving powerful forces dedicated to fanatical resistance to sexual union in all its varieties.

Five Baptist ministers entered Goldie's Book Shop—an adult bookstore—in order to "Just look around, and talk to some of the customers, maybe." When they got inside, they "saw filth and garbage." Young Jerry, a twenty-eight-year-old minister said that the acts depicted in Ms. Goldie's emporium were beyond anything he had ever experienced. (One would certainly hope so!) "It actually sickened my stomach. There were overt homosexuality, blatant lesbianism, sexual acts on the covers of books, color photographs of women with animals . . . We feel that filth and dirt belong in the gutter and that's where we put it!"

A passing policeman observed five males, aged eighteen to forty-four hurling magazines and books into the store's parking lot. All were arrested and charged with malicious mischief, vandalism, and destruction of private property. There is a strong hint in my mind that Young Minister Jerry is somehow related to Big Jerry the Probation Officer. I wonder how Hizzoner, Judge Sternly, will decide this one! Ms. Goldie, the offended party, was not available for comment, but I imagine her state of mind is similar to Abbie's door-slamming rage. Young Jerry, satisfied and proud in his martyrdom, is certain that he has struck a blow against the Devil. (The instigator of sexuality.) He sincerely believes that the pictures he threw into the gutter actually *cause* people to commit the sex act. This assumption is controversial at best. His basic premise that the sex act in itself is evil has had millions of adherents for many centuries in the history of human thought. This primal aversion to the union of the opposites is based on the fact that sexuality first manifested as an overwhelming urge to commit incest. When the young human first experiences erection and sexual lust for woman, the most visible objects for gratification are his mother and females in his immediate family. Freud's Oedipus conflict deals with this problem. Girls face the same problem as their natural bodies express the budding desire for union of the opposites. The incest taboo is the equally strong resistance which balances the vehement attraction between the opposite sexes. If the axiom that every man marries his mother, and every girl lusts after her father is accepted, we can begin to understand why antisexual union forces are called "vice squads."

"Hey, look at this article on the front page. It looks like women's lib is really making some changes!" Ben has been looking at the newspaper while I have been absorbed in my thoughts.

"An Alameda County judge ruled Thursday that the police practice of arresting prostitutes but merely issuing citations to their customers was discriminatory." Smiling broadly, he tells me about "This lady cop, about thirty years old, who stood on the corner dressed in red slacks and a blue sweater. In her purse was a handgun and a police badge. She was backed up by four plainclothes officers in two unmarked cars."

"I just sort of stand on the street curbs and look for a car to drive by twice," she says. "Usually he rolls down his window and I walk over, and he asks if I am a working girl and if I am looking for a little fun. He'll say 'I'm looking for a French,'or some other particular kind of sex act, and I'll bust him."

Ben wants to know why it is against the law to ask a girl if she wants to have a little fun. "I ask that question every time I meet a pretty girl. They don't seem to mind. They even seem to like it . . . It's only Abbie who really hates me." If convicted, the eight middle-class, white, suburbanite "customers" face a maximum penalty of six months in jail and a six hundred dollar fine.

"As it is they're in for a weekend in jail. The law requires a VD test which takes twenty-four hours . . . Those poor bastards were busted Friday night, and they won't even draw blood for the tests until sometime Monday."

"Their names and ages are in the paper and everything. One guy is forty-five, his friend is fifty-five, one is thirty-six. They even printed their addresses . . . I wonder what happened when their families found out." A picture of Tarot card #16, "The Blasted Tower," flashes across my mind's eye. "I really don't see why they're so hard on people who just want to have a little fun," says Ben as he leaves for his basketball game.

Finding myself alone, I arrange myself on the front porch and busy myself soaking up the warm California sun. It's a form of solar meditation. I call it The Lizard on the Rock pose. Relaxing in the warm, glowing sunlight, I close my eyes and focus the rays on my optic chiasm. As I think, "This should take me down to six.". . .

Theta appears and announces, "Actually, I'm just behind the optic chiasm. I'm in the pineal gland. That's your third eye. You see, I'm just a hologram, but so, for that matter, are you."

"And you're supposed to be teaching me how to drive it . . . Right?" I ask.

"Right," he replies. Theta is dressed in a yellow satin cape and wears a red skull cap. As I watch, he changes his costume a bit. The skull cap turns white as the cape turns black and grows a furry white trim around its edges. He makes the sign of a cross and Isis reappears in a black dress trimmed with white lace at the collar, sleeves, and edges. She looks about thirteen. She explains that she has chosen to reveal herself to me in this form for her own reasons. The form she has chosen is that of a cartoon character called Little Orphan Annie. "When we meet down on the planet, I will adopt the female form appropriate to the occasion." When I inquire as to the purpose of our impending meeting down on the planet, she giggles and says, "Just to have a little fun."

Abbie comes out onto the porch and interrupts my reverie to announce that she has a cold and a stuffy nose. "I guess that's why I was so grumpy." Popping herself into bed, she examines a tuning fork and wants to know why a doctor would use a thing like that.

"It's a way of testing for deafness." Thumping the tuning fork on a chair, I place it in the center of her forehead just below the hairline. The sound localizes to her left ear. "That means that the hearing is better in the other ear. The vibrations are carried to the ear through your skull bone. It seems louder in the left ear because there is less normal sound interfering with the bone transmission."

As if from nowhere, an idea springs fully formed into my mind. "Why couldn't a tuning fork be used as a source of energy for the sonopuncture treatments?" Skeptical as ever, Abbie agrees to allow me to stimulate her acupuncture points with the vibrating tuning fork. The stem of the instrument placed against three points on her foot, two on her wrist, and one on her forehead seemed to have no general effect. The hearing test was repeated. Immediately after the five-minute treatment she reported that the sound was equally distributed between her two ears. She freely admits the improvement but adamantly refuses to believe that the tuning fork had anything to do with it. I observe about two hours later that she seems to feel much better. Our little patient admits that she is greatly improved but is certain that "that sound mumbo-jumbo had nothing to do with it." (Two days later, sound distribution was equal in both ears, and her general condition continued to improve markedly.) Actually the tuning fork delivering vibratory energy at a rate of 128 cycles per second may be as effective as the million cycle per second ultrasound therapy head. It has the decided advantage of not depending on outside energy . . . A tuning fork doesn't have to be plugged in. When I tell her that she may have been a party to a great medical discovery (do it yourself sonopuncture) our little heroine shrugs and says, "Far out; get me a fresh roll of toilet paper . . . my nose is running."

The dog's barking announces the return of brother Ben who has brought an interesting letter along with today's mail. It is from a man named Dan Stat of Wilmington, Delaware.

"Enclosed is an article which describes an experience and investigation which I pursued last year relative to the ingestion of a specific sound developed by an ancient Peruvian civilization. I believe it has some relevance to work you are presently engaged in. I would be interested in your comments and anything which you have written regarding the effect of high frequency sound ingestion as a therapeutic technique."

He also believes that "the use of sound is only just beginning to be understood and we are on the threshold of the door to a whole new technology which will have wide-ranging effects on mankind."

The article, from the *Journal of Transpersonal Psychology* describes Dan's experience with a pre-Colombian whistling bottle from Peru which he picked up at an auction. It looks somewhat like a pottery chianti bottle attached by two hollow tubes to a hollow vessel, shaped into a figure. The actual sound is produced by a whistle in the upper connecting tube which doubles as a handle. One afternoon, his mind functioning at twenty-four cycles per second, he blew into the vessel's spout. Dropping down to thirteen, he thought about "the circumstances whereby the jug had been created and its possible place in the ancient culture which had created it." Without any further effort on his part, Dan's mind immediately shifted down to the alpha range. " . . . Thoughts disappeared as the vessel's sound filled my ears." The sound that he heard was forcing a sacred connotation which had neither been anticipated nor solicited. "It was akin to a mantra invoking a spiritual, emotional, and philosophical harmony with the universe."

"What does he mean by that?" Ben wants to know.

"He blew into this thousand-year-old bottle and got stoned."

"On the sound?"

"He wasn't sure." He took it over to the University of Pennsylvania Museum and was told it came from a highly advanced civilization called the Chimor Kingdom. It emits a pure tone which causes changes in blood pressure, heart rate and respiratory rate according to tests he had done at Hahnemann Medical College in Philadelphia.

"What's a mantra?"

"Mantras are sacred syllables spoken or chanted in religious ceremonies to evoke a spiritual experience or inspirational state," says the article. "A mantra is a sound or a chant that gets you stoned," I add. In response to his query as to the origin of the word "stoned," I offer the theory that it has some relation to *the lapis* (stone) of alchemy, which is described as "the panacea which heals all ills."

"Uh huh," says Ben in a tone which indicates to me that he is now completely engrossed in his copy of Mary Shelley's *Frankenstein*. "Did you know that she was married to that famous English poet with the same name . . . Shelley?"

Six days later as promised, Ms. Pixie materializes at the address in San Francisco which turns out to be the office of a large daily newspaper. Thirtyish, attractive, blonde and intelligent, she is interested in the therapeutic applications of sound ingestion. She wants to know, "Will sonopuncture alone cure disease? . . . How long does the improvement last?"

"Most healing," I hear myself telling her, "occurs in the alpha-theta state. In this state, the mind is functioning at a rate which shows up on the electroencephalogram as the range between four and twelve cycles per second. Administration of sound vibrations into the acupuncture system appears to induce symptom suppression in seventy to eighty percent of all patients so treated."

"Do you feel that symptom suppression is the same as, or equivalent to healing . . . achieving a cure?" I agree that it is not, but note that a great many patients are interested only in symptom relief and not in the effort involved in achieving healing or cure. "Doesn't a suppressed symptom tend to recur?"

"A symptom is a message. It will recur and change its form until such time as the patient makes the required change in lifestyle or thinking pattern. I think the sound is a device or ritual which helps the patient get into the alpha-theta state. Healing comes only from that which takes the patient beyond entanglement with the ego." The voice is mine; the words are those of Albert Karl.

Fusion of the Opposites

March 21, 1975. The first day of spring is announced on page one of the San Francisco *Chronicle:* MONSTER STORM STRIKES BAY AREA! The deluge washes away some roads, a house or two, electric power lines, about six million jobs. At the same time the Lon Nol government of Cambodia as well as that of South Vietnam are engulfed by a Red tide of humanity surging down from the north. The tidal wave of revolution sweeps down behind the swelling stream of refugees. By Good Friday the great storm of '75 is tearing at the last bastions of twentieth century reality. Desperation has led some to attempt the resurrection of Richard Nixon. The megacorporation, child of the industrial revolution, has been caught with its hand in the cookie jar. It begins to look like all those jokes about the United States Government being a subsidiary of ITT were right on the beam. The Good Friday NBC Evening News announces that Congress has set up a committee to look into the connection between the CIA and the assassination of President Kennedy. The Easter Sunday paper carries a cartoon showing two battered CIA operatives discussing the advisability of changing their image. The caption suggests that perhaps they should trade their trench coats in for strait jackets.

In the midst of the raging deluge, The Maharishi Mahesh Yoga appears at Civic Auditorium in San Francisco . . . "resembling a jovial little lion of heaven," and announces the dawn of the Age of Enlightenment. Later that same week, King Faisal of Saudi Arabia is "wasted" by a member of his closely knit family circle.

"How come," asks a reporter, "with war all over the place, and depression and inflation and crime, you claim an Age of Enlightenment is dawning?" The Maharishi replies in a voice which sounds like it is coming over a telephone that, "It's always darkest before the dawn. Dawn's inaugural ceremony must be done while it's still dark. Within a few weeks, a few months, the light will be all too apparent . . . Every dawn has a sunset ahead of it." The Palm Sunday edition of the San Francisco *Chronicle* carries a description of the role I am to play against this social backdrop. Ms. Pixie has written an article about a general practitioner "who retired four years ago at age 45. He directed the recently disbanded Headlands Healing Service, a clinic which specialized in unorthodox treatment for the four years of its operation." The doctor claims to have evolved a technique which he describes as "A breakthrough that surpasses the discovery of anesthesia and antibiotics." He says he uses sonopuncture in a way that relieves symptoms, but feels he has taken the system a step further, to reach the source of disease.

"Western medicine," he maintains, "treats symptoms as an enemy that needs to be repressed, but if you want to get healing, treat them as a friend and listen to what they have to say. Disease is the body's way of protesting . . . if a life adaptive pattern is destructive, illness requires that we cease and desist. If necessary, the body will create cancer to make us change. Symptoms are there to make us alter our lifestyle." He then describes a therapeutic approach he calls "Applied Alchemy." On reading this, I have the feeling that I have done all this sometime before, but I can't remember where or when.

The telephone bell interrupts my reverie.

"Hi," it says, "my name is Art." The voice states that it belongs to a journalist reporter who does a nightly radio show. "We reach the entire Western United States." He read

Ms. Pixie's article in the *Chronicle*. "I would like to talk about it on the air." Since I don't feel much like driving to San Francisco for a broadcast which runs from 8:00 P.M. until midnight, he will arrange to do it on the telephone. At 7:50 P.M. it rings again, and engages me in a two-hour conversation about healing. For openers, he wants to know, "I understand you refer to yourself as a healer. Did you actually say that if it was necessary you would dance around half-naked by the light of the full moon waving an eagle feather in order to get your patient well?"

"I did, but it was merely a figure of speech."

"I understand you use a beam of sound into the acupuncture system. Could you tell me how sticking a needle into the foot could possibly help a sore throat?"

"The same way putting a penicillin pill into your mouth helps a sore, infected toe." Art admits that he never realized or thought about the similarity. "It's entirely possible that all our supersophisticated twentieth century medical manipulations and procedures are nothing but high-class rituals."

The newsbreak on the hour reports the complete collapse of the South Vietnamese army. The Red Cross is in the process of kidnapping several thousand Vietnamese children, aided and abetted by the air force which killed their parents. The first batch has already been distributed to foster homes in the United States. The second batch wasn't as lucky. Their C-5A army transport crashed on take-off. A caller wants to know why the American Red Cross thinks white Anglo-Saxon protestants can provide better care for yellow skinned orphans than their own people could. Uncle Gerry, our beloved President feels, according to the news report, that we have a Sacred Christian Duty to save these children from the fate awaiting them at the hands of the onrushing yellow tide of North Vietnamese Reds. Vice President Rockefeller states that his mood is one of "black depression."

That black depression he's talking about is, of course, the black space in between the "on" flashes of the hologram. Alchemists called it the stage of blackness . . . "the nigredo." It is possible to see that a new golden age of man is arising out of the black lead of the Vietnam War. If the vice president plays his cards right, his depression will reverse its polarity and turn into pure joy. The two are, in a manner of speaking, flip sides of the same record. Like the theory of relativity says, it all depends on your point of view. There are two pair of opposing views of the current situation in Southeast Asia. The North Vietnamese government sees a "tremendous victory for the forces of humanity and justice" in what the South calls "an immense human tragedy." In the East, Mr. Rockefeller's Chinese counterpart expresses "great joy" on contemplating the events which precipitated the vice president's deep melancholia.

The sun rises in the East and sets in the West. This was ever so. It is fitting in this spring season that we see him abandoning the southern regions, and smiling with renewed favor upon the northern provinces. The opposites, just because *they are in conflict, will gradually draw together, and what looked like death and destruction will settle down into a latent state of concord, suitably expressed by the symbol of pregnancy. It seems that the pregnancy symbol indicates the imminent birth of a new civilization on the planet.*

The world, like the egg, is round. When the world was large, and its numbers few, humans tended to isolate themselves into groups, mixing only with their own kind, and hating all other kinds. Now, their numbers have greatly increased and they buzz around the planet at supersonic speed. The world egg has grown small indeed. All the aspects of humanity, black and white, red and yellow, capitalist and communist, find that on a shrinking planet, they can no longer avoid prolonged and constant intermingling.

They will pass through a stage where they try to kill each other off. The outcome of this struggle will be the realization of the One. In order to survive, the four races of humanity must accept their roles as composite parts of a single living organism. This organism is called the planet, the galaxy or the cosmos, depending on its level of organization.

The NBC Evening News continues . . . first group of Vietnamese orphans has arrived in the land of milk and honey.

They are mostly offspring of the union of black Western males with yellow Eastern females. Holding her new found daughter close in the primal embrace of motherhood, a young blonde California woman says, "If you save one child, you have saved the whole world." She plans to call her dark skinned daughter *Jennifer*.

The green telephone on the table rings. "My name is Jane," says the little green talking box. "I read about you in the paper and I was hoping you could help me." She is thirty-seven and an active sportswoman. "I've broken so many bones, that it doesn't even hurt anymore when I have a fracture." Her present complaint is severe, persistent pain in her shoulder. She stated that she had consulted an orthopedist who put her in traction, prescribed some pills and referred her to a neurosurgeon, in that order. "He took some x-rays and said I had a thoracic outlet syndrome. He says I need an operation, and nothing else will help my suffering. When I asked him if he thought wearing a sling under my arm would help he acted like it was an insult to his dignity; consulting him about something as picayune as a sling. The pain is driving me out of my mind. I don't want an operation, I don't want to take any more of those damned pills. I simply refuse to believe that I have no other choice. I will not accept their condemning me to a lifetime of torture and pain." She seems on the verge of tears.

"The nigredo," says a voice in my head, " the state of pregnancy." When I ask her if she can make pictures in her head she replies, "Of course, I'm an artist."

"Flash a picture in your mind's eye which represents the present condition of your body," I suggested.

"One half is all black," she replies in an instant.

"Fix the image in your mind and repair it."

"I've cut away the black half with an Exacto knife. I now have half a body." She is advised to concentrate on her breathing and ignore the thoughts that race through her head. "I know how to do Yogic breathing." She agrees to drive her half body to her summer home by the sea, concentrating only on her breathing and her driving. Upon arrival, she will sit by the sea, breathe, and create a whole, perfect body in her mind's eye.

The clock on the wall moves ahead four hours, and the green telephone's bell rings again. "It worked," says the voice calling itself Jane. "My body is completely new. I was able to visualize a perfect restoration. My body feels like it's whole again. I've thrown away my sling and I know I'll never have trouble with my shoulder again." My mind flashes a picture of a true believer waggling upraised palms. I inform her that she has only achieved symptom suppression which should not be confused with a "cure" or a "healing." To prevent recurrence of alternate symptoms on a higher level of suffering, she must understand the message inherent in her shoulder pain.

"How," she wants to know, "do I do that?"

"Think of your pain as energy which is stagnant. Close your eyes, breathe, and watch for someone or something to appear."

"I see a little girl! She's sitting there looking at me."

"Greet her, make friends with her and ask whether she knows about your shoulder pain. Ask her if it's a message . . . "

She says her name is *Jennifer*. She has been kicking me in the back because I've been hanging around with people she can't tolerate. She has been trying to call my attention to prevent my social and business obligations from stifling and suffocating her." Jennifer tells Jane that if she will arrange to withdraw from time/space for fifteen minutes daily they could plot a course through daily life which would be beneficial to both and harmful to neither. Mother and newborn daughter express their thanks as the telephone falls silent.

If you'll think back a few pages, you will recall that a holy man from the East recently announced the birth of a new age at the Civic Center in San Francisco. The dawn of the new age is always symbolized by the birth of a child.

"Only this time it's a girl," says Isis. *The old man poses a riddle. "What," he wants to know, "happens when an irresistible force meets an immovable object?" He immediately answers his own question. "As in the case of a collision be-*

tween a positron and an electron they annihilate each other. The result, as we perceive it, is an energy packet in the form of a flash of light. The new unity consists of two light quanta. The new unity," he proposes, "is the irresistible force and the immovable object after collision and fusion have taken place. The post-coital light flash is neither force nor object, yet it is simultaneously both."

Lao Tzu, in my mind's eye, looking inscrutable as usual, holds up a gaily colored easter egg (world egg). "This time, you see, it has been fertilized." In his other hand he holds a cardboard egg carton on the top of which has been inscribed the word: FERTILIZED. *"It is neither father nor mother, yet it is simultaneously both." He holds up another sign. This one says:* AT THIS POINT IT IS POSSIBLE TO ACHIEVE LIBERATION.

"He means," says Albert Karl, "that it is now possible to see the light." He laughs heartily at his joke. "The irresistible force is male, it moves, and it is yang. I like to symbolize it by the sperm which fertilized Lao Tzu's world egg. All those snakes and serpents you read about down there, they're really sperm. I'm thinking of writing a song called 'a worm is really a sperm.' In the lyrics is a subtle suggestion that the serpents on the caduceus are really a pair of sperm fighting to the death over right of passage into the egg. The egg is, of course, the immovable object.

The picture dissolves into a scene from Star Trek. *A black figure is locked in a death struggle with an identical white figure. Isis informs me that they are a pair of opposites locked in a space warp outside of time. "Primal, eternal enemies, locked in forever, with no hope of escape," she muses. "Male and female trapped on the planet. At first they will engage in total war, since they are natural enemies."*

"They have to be, since they're a pair of opposites." The old man now looks like he could be Isis' twin brother. He states that he is also her father and her lover, winking lewdly in her direction.

"You know what you are?" she snaps angrily at him. "You're nothing but a dirty old man!"

"That and much more, my dear," he leers back at her.

Glaring at him she adopts the attitude of a mother ignoring the antics of a naughty son. Turning her attention to the continuing battle of the opposites on the TV screen, she continues. "At first there is a terrible struggle for power, first the one gaining the upper hand, and then the other. The tide of battle swings back and forth throughout all eternity, with no hope of disengagement or victory for either side."

"Once you have introduced the element of intelligent, conscious thought, it is inevitable that the two combatants will realize the futility and the mutual destructiveness of continuing a battle in which any sort of victory for either side is clearly impossible. The wars end, and the combatants decide that they might as well try to live with each other, since the other alternatives are unthinkable."

The twins join hands. "At that point we always get married and live happily ever after, until he starts lusting after other women or whatever. He's always lusting after something or other."

"I can't help it. It's my nature." The two fuse and disappear in a flash of light and a puff of smoke.

The Road Show

As the connubial light flash fades, and I teeter on the edge of the twilight zone, Marty the Medical Director drives up in his red Fiat sports convertible. He has come to pick me up for a weekend healing conference.

"C'mon, get in," he says. I climb aboard, and we drive off into a rainstorm. It is the weekend of the new moon. Howling winds and driving rain buffet our little craft. Water begins to drip through the convertible top onto my lap. We soon arrive at a place which calls itself "Pajaro Dunes." Pajaro Dunes is a community of outlandishly expensive and elegant houses situated at the western edge of the Western world, on the Pacific Ocean. The way into the community is blocked by a green gate. Pulling up to a small square box on the left, Marty pushes a button and identifies himself. The gate slowly slides to our right and disappears. As we enter it reappears, blocking our exit.

A short drive, a board walk across white, rain drenched sand leads us to the door of house number 94. As we approach the house, a sudden gust of wind hurries up from the churning sea. The front door slowly swings ajar. Taking this to be a good omen, we enter, and begin searching for a place to deposit our luggage. Without warning, a female voice materialized somewhere in the space above my head.

"You guys," it says in a no-nonsense tone, "are in the wrong house. This is the Gestalt Women's Weekend house." Silently agreeing that we are in the wrong house, we beat a hasty retreat, passing hordes of human females busily engaged in carrying huge amounts of food into the building. They seem to be laying in a stock of provisions for some sort of new moon ritual.

After making inquiries and wandering around some, we arrive at the door to house #106. This is a five-bedroom palace so situated that looking out the windows or sitting on the porch gives one the distinct impression of being on a ship at sea. Among our fellow passengers are two Ph.D.s named David, a neurologist named Norman and a cancer curer called Carl. Also present upon our arrival was a cancer curee named Don. Norman and Carl are M.D.s: Don is rich. A nice looking woman, about sixty, who says her name is Djeane, has cornered Carl on the couch, and is busily extracting words from his head, stuffing them into a tape recorder through a small black phallus. She says it's a microphone. As we enter the room she turns to face me. I become aware at once that the right side of her face is flat, motionless, and host to a single, unblinking blue eye.

"I have Bells Palsy," says the left side of the face. "I have also cured myself of cancer." She is collecting the words of Carl "in order to spread them around where they will do the most good." At 6:00 P.M. she stuffs her bundle of words into a brown leather pouch, waves goodbye and disappears down the wooden walkway.

From the conversation which follows, I gather that Carl, a thirty-two-year-old radiologist, has aroused the ire of some of his colleagues by helping a significant number of his terminal patients achieve cancer cures through a technique involving visual imagery. He has apparently been teaching them to reprogram their holograms by means of the alpha-theta technique which I learned back on the space platform. "There's a rumor going around," joked David, the director of acupuncture research, "that certain members of the American Cancer Society are launching a special fund raising campaign. They are trying to raise the money to take out a contract on Carl." Carl, for his part, doesn't think it's funny. He does confirm the fact that certain members of the ACS are very annoyed at the suggestion that the ridiculously simple technique which he is investigating actually cures cancer. They have begun to throw around words like "quack" and "rip-off artist."

"They say I'm raising false hope in the minds and hearts of terminal patients. That's a contradiction in terms. How can hope be false?" A knock on the door announces the presence of a young man who calls himself "Ananda."

"Is that your first name or your last name?" someone asks.

"It's a name I got from my Indian guru." He is a graduate student at Lone Mountain College in San Francisco. His grade advisor has suggested that he check in with the staff at the healing conference before submitting to surgery. His orthopedic surgeon performed an orthogram on his knee and demonstrated a torn cartilage. The orthopedic guru has recommended removal of the torn cartilage.

"He wanted to operate even before he did the orthogram," says the disciple. "I read your book, *The Healing Mind,* in which you suggest that it might be possible to heal this thing without surgery." He really seems skeptical and torn between two worlds; the world of his half-naked heathen guru and the white gowned, sterile world of his orthopedic surgeon. His heathen Indian guru instructed him to "stay in the center." He understands this to mean that he must follow a middle course which leads between the clashing opposites. His orthopedic surgeon feels that "Unless this torn cartilage is repaired it will cause further degeneration in the surrounding tissues in the future." Ananda had an x-ray image of the problem knee. To Ananda it looks like a shadowgram of a large cross-cut saw. "One of the teeth has worked itself loose and is just hanging there."

Ananda is obviously in the throes of The Great Paradigm Clash. The diagnosis and prognosis of the orthopedic surgeon are stretching to the limit his faith in the words of the dirty little heathen dwarf. He is caught in his hologram! The way out, as I now know, leads through the alpha-theta state. Stepping out of the hologram for a moment (dropping into alpha) I experience the thought that I am still doing general practice. I am being confronted with a patient who has to deal with diametrically opposite opinions after consulting two eminent specialists. He is obviously suffering from an overdose of orthopedic-surgeon-type energy and needs an equal dose of Indian guru energy to restore his balance and allow him to make an intelligent decision regarding his degenerating time/space knee.

"Can you make a picture of your guru in your head?" Yes, he can. He makes a picture of the guru in the neural field between his optic nerve crossing and his pineal gland. I presume he has shifted into theta. For my part, I hold to my picture of a patient entering the theta state. "I am now going to speak with your picture of your guru. When I ask a question, just tell me the first answer which flashes into your mind." He agrees to the procedure. "O. K. Question one is, does the guru know about the problem manifesting in Ananda's knee?"

Ananda is silent for only a moment. "Yes, he does."

"Is he sending you a message?"

"Yes, he is."

"What is the message?"

Ananda is silent for a full minute. "He says that I am too earthbound." The guru agrees with my provisional diagnosis. We are dealing with a textbook picture of the *Narcissus Syndrome,* a common pathologic condition in which the patient becomes trapped in his hologram and loses complete control of it. This diagnosis in no way conflicts with the prognosis of the orthopedic surgeon. His prophecy of continued degeneration of the time/space body in the absence of definitive therapeutic procedures seems to me accurate.

"How can Ananda be less earthbound?" I ask the apparition. There is no response. I have the distinct feeling that I am dealing with Albert Karl in one of his infinite forms. I suggest to Ananda that he meditate for a period of fifteen minutes one to three times daily and consult with the guru in the hope that he will provide an answer to the riddle.

"My orthopedic surgeon is away for the next week." The patient will spend that time in daily consultation with the guru. He leaves after expressing his thanks.

A moment later he pops his head in the door to tell us a story about his guru. "I don't know why I thought of it just now, but I feel I should tell you this parable." In the course of conversation, Ananda asked his guru. "What is death?"

"I don't know," replied the guru.

"But if you're a guru you should know!"

"While it is true that I am a guru, it is not true that I am a dead guru."

"I suppose what he means by that," says the program co-ordinating person, who has just arrived, "is don't knock it until you've tried it."

"An interesting point of view," notes Carl the cancer curer. "I find that my cancer patients are always people who have chosen to die rather than change their belief structure."

"To die for one's beliefs is a very admirable act," says the coordinating chairperson, who looks very familiar to me. I know I have met this person before. The feeling of déjà vu (already seen) becomes intense as I study the speaker. Fine, strong features, Afro hair style, about thirty-three.

"Until I started working with cancer patients, I didn't understand that some patients actually choose death. I didn't understand that at all," comments Carl. "I knew that there was some factor which I couldn't explain which had a lot to do with the outcome of their disease." The clue came for Carl when he came across the "surveillance theory" of immunology. This theory holds that the human body is continuously creating malignancies which are constantly being destroyed by the body's defense system. Cancer only kills us when we literally drop our guard and allow it to run riot and cause death. The white blood cells which are alleged to destroy invading bacteria perform the same function when they come across rapidly dividing cancer cells . . . according to this theory. "This totally changed my belief structure regarding the phenomenon of cancer. It is not necessary to destroy all the cancer cells; it is only necessary to reactivate the patients' defenses and shift the struggle in their favor.''

He describes his technique whereby the patient images a cure, or more specifically, he images his body defenses destroying the tumor. According to his preliminary results, the body responds and destroys the malignancy.

"It's the same as leaving the room to take a leak," notes Norman the neurologist. I get the signal from my full bladder, make a mental image of myself emptying it into the latrine, and my body does the rest simply and efficiently without my having to think about it.'' He gets up and leaves the room. We all wait patiently for him to return. "As my body was leaving the room and emptying its bladder, I was thinking about the problem of the nature of the human will. My body carried out emptying in direct response to the stretch reflex arising in the bladder wall. How was my *will* able to make it go through the ritual of leaving the room? We know absolutely nothing about the manner in which my volition is able to initiate activity in the nerves which inhibit bladder emptying.''

"How, for that matter, did you get your body to come back into this room, sit down, and continue our conversation?'' The program chairperson giggles, giving away her identity. She has chosen the form of a farm girl cocktail waitress from Ohio who has brought us all together as part of a course on healing.

"It's all a matter of relaxation and visualization," says Carl. He cites a case history using his technique.

"He was a sixty-year-old man with advanced throat cancer. First I had him relax as much as he possibly could. This was easier if he pictured himself in a tranquil, peaceful place. When he felt that his mind was completely at peace, he was to picture his cancer as it appeared to him. The nature of the mental image he created was unimportant. It was only necessary that the mental image represent the cancer as it appeared in his mind's eye. A word description works just as well . . . you could even say "it looks like a lump of shit" and it would work. He pictured a bunch of maggots devouring the lump of shit. That was his picture of, and command to, his efficiently operating autoimmune defense system. He did this for fifteen minutes three times a day. Six weeks later his cancer was gone!"

"He commanded his body to destroy the cancer and it responded the same efficient and obedient way in which my hand responded to my command to zip up my fly and check it once before I came into the room." Norman the neurologist has come a long way since the days when he ripped people's spines open in order to make their feet stop hurting.

"This was totally surprising to me . . . I could not explain what had happened." Carl was completely blown out by the clinical response to his unorthodox therapeutics.

"I, myself, am considering publication offers on my new book *Occult Medicine Can Save Your Life,*" notes Norman Neurologist, M.D., with a knowing smile. He understands why Carl spent the next four years trying to see how often he could make it happen again.

"I find that it's a damned hard thing to do . . . I find it hard to overcome my colds." Someone suggests to Carl that he might find his life easier if he spent more time understanding things instead of overcoming them. Carl shows slight irritability. "It was hard for me to understand how I had created my own symptoms . . . let alone cancer patients." His manner betrays the fact that it is still hard for him to relinquish his father's belief structure. "When you are right in the middle of being ill, right in the throes of the disease, it's hard to step back and appreciate what the message is. That," he continues with rising emotion, "is very threatening . . . very frustrating. It seems to make the illness even worse." At this point Carl Cancer Curer, M.D., does a complete turnabout; he reverses his polarity. "It is, however, not impossible, and for those who can accomplish it, it is a most gratifying procedure . . . to become an active participant in what's going on."

"The key seems to lie in the belief system of the individual," notes Norman Neurologist.

"Most of my patients," continues Carl, "came to me with the firm belief that they had no control over their cancer . . . that it came upon them from out of the blue, and that it probably was going to kill them. They were convinced that there wasn't a heck of a lot they could do about it, but they were willing to clutch at this particular straw." He suggested to his patients that if their physical condition was getting worse, perhaps their belief structure was somehow evolving in a destructive direction. "It's sort of a biofeedback mechanism. Then, instead of locking horns with the disease, it becomes possible to listen to the message it carries . . . these are the things that need to be changed, and these are the areas in which the change has to be made." Carl suggests to his patients that when they live with their disease, and increase their awareness of that disease, it is easy to tell the direction in which the disease is moving . . . "primarily by how you feel. If you feel inner peace, your disease will resolve and regress; if your sense of inner agitation increases, your symptoms get worse."

Releasing one's hold on the parental belief structure is an act which requires uncommon faith and even a touch of heroism. A story illustrates the point. A man was standing on the edge of a sheer precipice when the ground gave way beneath his feet. As he went over the edge he recalled with horror that the drop at this point on the cliff was some two thousand feet straight down. Glancing downward he was aware that the foot of the cliff was shrouded in mist so that the end of his fall was not visible. Something brushed against his hand and he clutched frantically at what turned out to be a stout rope attached to a firmly rooted shrub about two hundred and fifty feet down. His fall was broken, but ascent was clearly impossible. Some form of outside assistance was absolutely essential to his survival.

"Is there anyone up there?" he shouted at the mountain top and at the heavens above his head.

The response came from heaven above in the form of a voice. "Yes, my son," said the celestial speaker. "I am up here."

"Can you help me?"

"DO YOU HAVE FAITH?"

"Sure, what do you want me to do?"

"LET GO OF THE ROPE."

After a long silence, the man says, "Is there anyone else up there?"

Our chairperson dissolves into peals of laughter which arrange themselves into the sound of a running brook . . . she really likes that story. "I'd like to do a theater piece which would blow out the audience . . . Encourage them to let go of the rope." She cracks up and dissolves into a pool of giggles. "I'd like it to be a healing seminar that really heals."

The performance took place at the Del Mar Theatre in Santa Cruz before an audience of about fifteen hundred paying customers ($45 per ticket). A significantly large percentage of the audience were doctors, psychiatrists, healers, psychics and various other health professionals. Carl Cancer Curer, M.D., did his bit exactly as described above. The audience loves it. David Director of Acupuncture Research at The Medical School, Ph.D., played guitar, and did a Chinese soft shoe number called Tai Chi Ch'uan. For an encore he hypnotized everyone into believing that their hands are stuck together with magnetic glue. His act was a great success also.

Big Don knocked 'em dead with his home movies of a Filipino healer shoving his hands into the abdomen of a corpulent American Midwestern Matron, who, for her part, was smiling broadly and chatting amiably. Morris, the projectionist, had problems with his projector, so the film jumped around quite a bit adding a nice touch of informality to the performance. Big Don concluded his act with a well-documented case history . . . his own. He consulted the neurosurgical staff at Stanford University for a complaint of steadily increasing pain in his head. Examination revealed the presence of a brain tumor in the region of the pituitary gland. The neurosurgeons gave big Don two choices. A four- to six-hour brain operation, or certain death. While he was trying to decide between these two unpalatable choices, a friend told him about a psychic surgeon in the Philippines who had performed miraculous cures on reputable American citizens. Don bought a ticket and went to consult the healer.

"I met him in a hotel and told him my story. He said he could help me, took me upstairs to one of the rooms, laid me on the bed, shoved his fingers into my intact skull and pulled out what looked like a bunch of animal entrails, washed his hands and said it was finished. That was almost a year ago. Since then I have had no more headaches, and my neurosurgeon tells me he can't find the tumor." Don got a fine round of applause. His presentation may even have dented a few belief structures.

I hope this book has done the same. The seminar, first in a series of explorations into the nature of empirical reality as it relates to the healing process, also explored holographic theory. I should like to conclude this volume with a consideration of the hologram. The implications of this awesome new technology may well stretch your mind to the point where you will have to let go of the rope of your current belief structure. Let it go, give it up. The recently discovered characteristics of congruent laser light force us to consider the unheard of, and to think the inconceivable. This is best done in a relaxed, open state of mind.

Holographic theory is, according to some thinkers, one of the fundamental principals that one must grasp in order to understand new-age reality. Holography concerns the behavior of light when all its waves are congruent; that is, when they are all vibrating at the same frequency. You know what light is. It's that stuff that wriggles in at us from the sun. You can't see light. Light traveling through space is invisible. We are told that it consists of a wave in the universe; a wave which is also a particle. A beam of light whose wave particles are all vibrating at the same rate will weld a human retina back onto the eyeball, burn a hole in a sheet of steel, or bounce off the moon. It can carry millions of messages, and possibly even carries impulses through nerves. These beams of congruent light are called laser beams. It takes a pair of laser beams to create a three-dimensional image in space, just as it takes a pair of eyes to create the impression of a three-dimensional reality in space. The beams strike an object from two different directions. When they bounce off the object, they interact to create a new wave form. If you stick a photographic plate in the path of a combined wave an image is produced. The photographic image, called the hologram has some startling properties. If you cut the plate in half, each half will still contain the entire picture. If you cut it into a million pieces, each piece will still contain the total image of the object which was photographed. The total image is composed of an infinite number of smaller images of the same thing. This should illuminate the meaning behind the words of the Buddhist teacher who held up his staff saying: "If you understand this, you understand everything." It is also interesting to contemplate the hermetic admonition which states simply, "As above, so below." The whole is always contained in each of its parts.

Let me give you an example from my own field of medical practice. Suppose we presume the whole to be the human body. In anatomy classes, I dissected this gross physical body and gained some knowledge of its structure. Under the microscope, we see that each cell is as complex and mysterious as the entire body. On both levels we can see alternating periods of activity and quiescence. Each cell takes in food and excretes waste. Body and cell, that which is above and that which is below, live, mature, reproduce and die. Although each seems a separate unit, it actually is part of a larger whole which faithfully reflects it. In therapeutics, we apply this principle by altering the condition of the patient, through manipulation of one of the body's systems . . . in pneumonia, for instance, I alter the chemical composition of the blood stream by adding an antibiotic. This biochemical maneuver is reflected on the microscopic level by a decrease in the number of living pneumococcal germs. On the tissue level, it manifests as a decrease in swelling and congestion of the lungs. On the gross physical level we see a drop in fever, and the abatement of the signs of severe illness. On the level of consciousness, the patient says "I feel better." Since each unit is contained in all its parts, change in one changes all. By changing the state of the body we change consciousness.

The reverse is also true! A change in consciousness, the abandonment of a cherished belief structure, for example, manifests as a change in bodily state . . . as we have already seen.

One of the cherished beliefs we are now being asked to give up is the idea that we are skin and capsulated egos trapped in a real world of separately existing things. Here again, holographic theory sheds some light on our considerations. If you shine a beam of light through an ordinary photograph as in the case of a film strip, you need a screen to stop the image and reflect it back at you. In the absence of a reflecting surface, the beam travels out into infinite space. Not so with a hologram. If you pass a beam of light through a photographic plate containing the hologram, the resultant image interacts with the light waves in the room, to produce a three-dimensional image—in mid-air so to speak. The image is in 3-D and in color and appears to be what we call "real." Walk up to it and touch it. You find that there isn't anything there. Your senses have deceived you. What you perceive to be a real object in space is nothing but trapped light. Einstein's $E = MC^2$ leads us to the same conclusion. *What you perceive to be a real object in space is nothing but trapped light.* There are many who believe that this light which crystallizes as objects in space is identical with your own consciousness. To my knowledge, there are no reputable scientists around today who claim to understand the ultimate nature of light . . . what it actually is.

Next time you have a free day or so, even an hour will do, you can secretly exercise your belief structure. As you idly examine the world around you, consider the possibility that light and consciousness are one invisible and indivisible reality. The mind with which you examine the world, and the light by which you perceive it, are one and the same thing.

Afterword

Vence, France, 1976 May

O.K. Now let's really get back to reality . . . Come down to earth so to speak. Before we can do that, we must of course define what we mean by reality. Let me give you an example. As I look out my window I see a tree silhouetted against white walls and pink tile roof. If I shut my left eye, the scene instantly changes. It becomes flat, like the picture postcard of the same scene on my desk. If I then open my left eye as I shut the right one, the whole scene suddenly jumps toward my right! Not only does it move, but it changes radically. If you would like to try this simple experiment, I think you will be truly surprised. The left eyed view of the world differs markedly from the right eyed view of the world. By repeating the experiment with my glasses off, I can become aware of six different visual versions of the reality which exists outside, at any given instant. This data must pose a problem for any thinking person. If your reality testing mechanism breaks down you are considered crazy.

It is generally accepted common sense that "seeing is believing " I will believe that the chirping noises I hear outside are real birds if I look out the window and *see* them. (Maybe that's why blindness is feared more than any other disability by most people.)

Which of these six visual impressions am I to consider to be the real one? All my life, I have presumed that the view of my world with both eyes open and corrective lenses perched upon my nose is the most correct representation of that world. What then, am I to make of the amazing implications of a statement by a particle physicist, one Fritjof Capra when he implies that it is possible . . . "that the basic structures of the physical world are determined ultimately by the way in which we look at this world."

"That's ridiculous," you may reply. "It's the other way around. The world creates our view of it." Measure this notion against the evidence cited by Dr. John Ross (Chapter III) that your binocular visual system can produce three-dimensional squares where there is nothing but a bunch of blinking lights. How about your own experience on page 85, where your visual system produced borders and triangles in the absence of any real external stimulus? Look at those borders again and consider the words of the Buddhist teacher named Ashvaghosha.

"All phenomena in the world are nothing but the illusory manifestation of the mind and have no reality of their own."

While I may be forced to concede that the squares and the oblongs have no existence of their own, that in no way implies that all phenomena of the world are illusory. The tree and the building outside my window, for example, don't they exist on their own, independently of me? Dr. Capra states that there is a theory in his field of particle physics called the "bootstrap theory." This theory, he maintains, . . . "reflects the impossibility of separating the scientific observer from the observed phenomena. . . in its most extreme form it implies ultimately that the structures and phenomena we observe in nature (in our case the tree and building), are nothing but creations of our measuring and categorizing mind." In his *Tao of Physics*, he quotes another Buddhist sage named Yogacara who agrees. "These things people accept as an external world . . . what appears to be external does not exist in reality. It is indeed mind . . . nothing but mind." The three-dimensional images of a nonexistent square and a theoretically separately existent tree outside my window are formed from the fusion of two different monocular images, one image from each eye. This fusion apparently takes place in your visual cortex . . . the cortex being the unquestioned domain of the mind.

We may still maintain that the mind-created images are in the final analysis formed as a result of stimulation from something outside the mind itself. If so, of what are they composed that makes them different from me? Well, the building is made of bricks, the tree of plant cells and we humans of animal cells. On close examination, this hypothesis breaks down completely. Building, tree, and me, are all composed of molecules which are composed of atoms. Smashing up these atoms, we find that they fly apart into components which have the disturbing habit of going on and off as they change from matter into energy and back again into "particles." We can explain this strange behavior if we postulate that these subatomic particles are composed of quarks which by their arrangement create the particles which by their interactions create in turn atoms, molecules, building, tree and me. The only problem is that although fundamental particles (called *hadrons*) behave exactly as if they consisted of quarks, no one has ever demonstrated one. "According to the basic ideas about particle interactions quarks cannot exist." So says Dr. Fritjof Capra. This would imply that we live in a world of real, separately existing "things" which are composed of nonexistent building blocks . . . How is that possible?

We seem to be on the horns of paradox. We must admit that there is a solid real world outside my window which exists only in my mind! Science tells us that there is no fundamental substance; no primary, indivisible unit . . . no final, irreducible *thing. Everything is made out of nothing* (quarks). It seems to be characteristic of the rational mind to come up with this kind of solution to any problem which we pose. This state of affairs is beautifully illustrated by a story about an African god named Edsu. In order to teach the inhabitants about reality, he would appear in human form wearing a hat which was black on one side and white on the other. He would walk through the village looking straight ahead, speaking to no one. Heated arguments, even leading to bloodshed, would develop between those who saw the stranger in the white hat and those who saw the stranger in the black hat. Edsu would look down and laugh uproariously. Black or white, real or mind-created, it all depends on which side of the street you happen to stand. Reality, as Einstein pointed out in his theory of relativity, depends on your point of view. The experiment with the six realities outside my window tends to support this viewpoint. *All opposing viewpoints are equally true.* One must merely find a point of view which resolves the apparent paradox. A story illustrates:

Two men were loading a large crate onto a ship. Across the top were written the words *"This Side Up"* Painted under the words was a very large arrow pointing toward the bottom of the crate. Asked to explain the men replied, "It's O.K. this crate is from China." Inside the crate was a key, which bore the inscription:

DO NOT SEEK THE TRUTH . . .
ONLY CEASE TO CHERISH OPINIONS

This key was five thousand years old when you were born . . . it was three thousand years old when Christ was born. Scientists still use it. Nowadays we call it the "scientific attitude." The scientific attitude requires impartial observation of phenomena. Many people experience nature through the distorting lens of a belief structure; i.e., I am absolutely certain that hat was black (white).

Statements about the nature of reality made by people who *know* how it is, must be approached with extreme caution.

BOOKS OF RELATED INTEREST

THE HEALING MIND, controversial, fascinating first book by noted lecturer and medical researcher Dr. Irving Oyle, describes what is known about the mysterious ability of the mind to heal the body. 128 pages, soft cover, $5.95

Stanley Krippner and Alberto Villoldo's **REALMS OF HEALING** presents a scientific exploration of non-medical healing, and healing and healers, around the world, with emphasis on current laboratory research in the USA, USSR, Brazil and Canada. 252 pages, soft cover, $7.95

THE PAIN GAME by Dr. C. Norman Shealy, internationally known neurosurgeon, explains the physical and psychological sources of pain and how to deal with it. His emphasis throughout is on restoring mind and body to optimal health and fitness. 156 pages, soft cover, $4.95

THE COMPLETE BOOK OF ACUPUNCTURE by Dr. Stephen T. Chang offers the basic philosophy and practical applications of acupuncture for the layman and the physician. The text covers the flow of energy theory, common acupuncture points and treatment for internal diseases. 264 pages, soft cover, $7.95

NATURAL SOURCES by Moira Timms and Zachariah Zar is a holistic approach to nutrition, diet and health and offers a commonsense guide to Vitamin B—17 and its role in cancer prevention. 156 pages, soft cover, $4.95

HEALTH, YOUTH AND BEAUTY THROUGH COLOR BREATHING by Linda Clark and Yvonne Martine presents an exciting new technique to help readers stop the clock of physical aging and look, feel and act as they did in their twenties.
96 pages, soft cover, $4.95

ACKNOWLEDGMENTS

"Getting Even" © 1991 by Lee K. Abbott. First published in *Southwest Review*. Reprinted by permission of the author.

"Alamogordo" © 1991 by Cathryn Alpert. First published in *Puerto del Sol*. Reprinted by permission of the author.

"How I Came West, and Why I Stayed" © 1991 by Alison Baker. First published in *The Atlantic*. Reprinted by permission of the author.

"DeRay" © 1990, 1991 by Ron Carlson. First published in *Gentlemen's Quarterly*. Reprinted by permission of the author.

"The Mouse" © 1991 by Susan M. Gaines. First published in *The Missouri Review*. Reprinted by permission of the author.

"One-Eyed Jacks" © 1991 by Frances Stokes Hoekstra. First published in *Virginia Quarterly Review*. Reprinted by permission of the author.

"Lightning" © 1991 by David Long. First published in *The Sewanee Review*. Reprinted by permission of the author.

"What Happened to Tully" © 1991 by Tom McNeal. First published in *The Atlantic*. Reprinted by permission of the author.

"Around the World" © 1991 by Mary Morris. First published in *Crosscurrents*. Reprinted by permission of the author.

"The Ditch Rider" © 1991 by Kent Nelson. First published in "Shenandoah. Reprinted by permission of the author.

"Utah" © 1991 by Vince Passaro. First published in *Story*. Reprinted by permission of the author.

"It's Come to This" © 1991 by Annick Smith. First published in *Story*. Reprinted by permission of the author.

"The Way People Run" © 1991 by Christopher Tilghman. First published in *The New Yorker*. Reprinted by permission of the author.

"The Lake District" © 1991 by Evan Williams. First published in *Northwest Review*. Reprinted by permission of the author.

"Painted Pony" © 1991 by Dwight Yates. First published in *Quarterly West*. Reprinted by permission of the author.